THE CRIES AND APPEALS OF AFGHAN

Engineer Fazel Ahmed Afghan, MSc

To order additional copies of this book, contact:
Xlibris
844-714-8691
www.Xlibris.com
Orders@Xlibris.com

ISBN: Softcover   978-1-6698-5048-9
        Hardcover   978-1-6698-5049-6
        EBook   978-1-6698-5047-2

Print information available on the last page

Rev. date: 10/20/2022

THE CRIES AND APPEALS OF AN AFGHAN

CONTENTS

ABOUT THE AUTHOR

Engineer Fazel Ahmed Afghan, son of Mr. Abdul Satar Khan Popalzai (Durani), was born in 1937 in Salihan, District of Panjwai in Kandahar, Afghanistan. Ahmed Afghan completed his primary and secondary education at Habibia High School and the Afghan Institute of Technology (AIT) in Kabul, Afghanistan, in 1960.

He received his Bachelor's degree from the Faculty of Engineering at Kabul University in 1964. In 1972, he received his Master's degree in Structural Engineering from the University of Manitoba in Canada.

Ahmed Afghan has served in various positions within the construction division of the Ministry of Education, Kabul, Afghanistan. His primary duties included being in charge of building schools across the country.

He started by working tirelessly as an engineer, head of the engineering department, technical director, vice president and the President of the Construction division. Then, as the founder of the Construction Unit, he earned the honour of being the General President of the Construction Unit at the Ministry of Education in Kabul.

Ahmed Afghan has been the project coordinator for school buildings and similar projects financed by UNESCO, UNICEF, WFP, World Bank, and USAID in the Ministry of Education in Kabul. He was appointed Consul General of Afghanistan in Bombay, India, where he served from 1981 to 1985.

While living in India, Afghan continued working on his goal of establishing peace in his motherland, Afghanistan. He and his family settled in Vancouver, B.C., Canada, in Sept 1987, where he now continues to work toward his dear and critical goal of seeing a free and prosperous Afghanistan.

Ahmed Afghan's literary work includes:

1. **Master's degree thesis**: "A one–quarter scale experimental study of the effect of peripheral reinforcement in a concrete hollow-block shear wall." - April 1972, in (English)
2. **Educational building report for UNESCO**: "Innovation in the management of primary school construction in Afghanistan," (English)
3. **A book:** "My cries and appeals to the world leaders to bring about peace in beloved motherland Afghanistan," - 1985, (English)
4. **A documented and pictorial history book:** "Afghanistan from Heaven to Hell (1700 - 2001)"افغانستان از ثریا به قهقرا" in (Persian, Dary) which exposes the Conspiracies and Atrocities from 1700 - 2000.
5. **He had written a Hundred letters** to the world leaders as well as Political, Social and cultural articles and proposals for bringing peace to Afghanistan and unity among all his Afghan brothers and sisters (Dary).
6. **Documented and pictorial 700-page book** written in 2011, in (Dary) under the title "Cry of Afghan."
7. **A book:** Conspiracies and Atrocities in Afghanistan, 1700-2014 in 800 pages published in 2015, in (English).
8. **A book: About "Emagenary** Durand Line" titled the Conspiracies of British and Russia - 2022, in (Persian).
9. **An Autobiography:** The Autobiography and memoir of Engineer Fazel Ahmed Afghan, MSc.

Now, he lives without his late wife, Zahra Ahmed. However, Ahmed Afghan is very proud of his three daughters, one son, and seven grandchildren, who give him hope for a better future daily.

Author's Collections

1

2

3

4

5

6

7

8

9

HOMAGE AND CONDOLENCE

In The Name Of Allah, The Beneficent, The Merciful

I would like to express my humble tributes with a heavy heart and great respect to all the martyred Afghan brothers and sisters who are not with us anymore. I also want to mention all those who lost their precious lives fighting for our beloved motherland, Afghanistan. I pray for their souls to rest in peace in paradise.

I share my profound and deepest grief with all the bereaved families who have lost their dear and heroic family members in different parts of our country in never-ending, cruel, imposed wars since 1978.

As a human and a Muslim man who knows God created us to love each other, I extend my condolences to those bereaved families in other countries. They have received the bodies of their loved ones in boxes due to the last 44 years of imposed war in Afghanistan.

I express my most profound sorrow for those who have lost their state of mind during the imposed wars in Afghanistan.

I also express my sorrow for those who have lost their family members, limbs, shelters, and beloved motherland, forced to live abroad in depression.

May God the Almighty bless all my respected Afghan brothers and sisters who are unfortunately handicapped or addicted to heroin and other illegal drugs.

Also, I want to extend my love and respect for all those who were inhumanely humiliated. Furthermore, I want to reach out to those who lost their loved ones or precious lives due to hunger and different types of explosions during the bloodshed.

At last, I express my sympathies to all my Afghan sisters and brothers; they have lost all their social, economic, political and military achievements in the previous 20 years, from 2001 to August 15th, 2022.

DEDICATION

To my dear and honourable parents, may their souls be at peace in heaven as they raised me with great affection and encouraged me to attain higher education.

To my late beloved wife, Zahra Ahmed, and my dearest daughters, my son, sons-in-law, daughter-in-law, and grandchildren for their continuous encouragement, kind words, and loving support. Without them, it would have been tough for me to accomplish my work.

I also want to mention the late Dr. Ali Ahmed Popal, the father of education in Afghanistan. He was the one who believed in me and helped me continue my education. He encouraged me to go to the Afghan Institute of Technology in Kabul and the Engineering faculty at Kabul University.

Next, I want to dedicate this book to all my dear Afghan brothers and sisters who lost their precious lives fighting and struggling for freedom and peace.

All my Afghan brothers and sisters are continuously struggling and working hard to end the imposed injustice, crisis and bloodshed for the cause of bringing peace and justice to our beloved country, Afghanistan.

I hope the present and future Afghan generations, who are the inspiration of their parents and ancestors, will keep up the voice of freedom and unity of the Afghans, democracy, the country's integrity, and peace in independent Afghanistan.

I also want to dedicate this to the scholars who have devoted their lives in service of the public to promote and provide a sound education for the conscientious, sensible, intellectual and progressive children of Afghanistan.

Finally, this is for all my honourable and esteemed teachers and instructors who have educated me. Without their hard work and compassion, it would have been impossible for me to write this book.

Lastly, I want to shout out to all those brave people who exposed the internal and external conspiracies and atrocities in Afghanistan. I hope you continue working hard and remaining devoted to this honourable cause.

PREFACE

After graduating from the engineering faculty in 1964, I joined the Ministry of Education. It was my hope and passion to build schools for the sons and daughters of my beloved country while utilizing various internal and external sources of financial assistance.

I accomplished my dreams and ambitions with encouragement from my superiors and persistent hard work. Unfortunately, after the bloody coup d'etat in April 1978, everything changed. I was fired from duty as the president of the construction unit on the grounds of being in the United States and Canada to pursue my practical training and higher education (MSc). I also had financial assistance from Western governments and organizations to construct school buildings, which was another factor against me.

However, after two months, I was officially invited by UNESCO's Regional Office for Education in Bangkok, Thailand, to join the regional conference. They requested me to attend the conference and speak about my educational building report under "Innovation in the Management of Primary School Construction in Afghanistan." With this invitation, I was appointed as the general director of school mapping in the Ministry of Education planning division so I could attend the conference officially.

After the unjustified and bloody invasion of my motherland, Afghanistan, by the Soviet Union in December 1979, I was under the strict supervision of communist spies, and all the external financial assistance I had worked hard to construct school buildings frozen. Most of the existing schools and the schools under construction have been destroyed, leaving the children with no means of gaining education

Therefore, Dr. Anahita Ratibzad, the new minister of education, ordered me to return to the construction unit and start my work again. Furthermore, she asked me to try and re-encourage the inflow of foreign assistance for the education sector. Since it was an order, I had no choice but to accept the job, despite initially rejecting it reluctantly.

However, an incident soon made me realize the severity of losing our sovereignty as a nation and as individuals.

One day, I went to the minister's office for some instructions. While I waited outside the office for permission to enter and meet her, a Russian adviser barged into the office without permission and left after a few minutes. I was pretty bewildered watching this unfold. After I got the opportunity to enter the minister's office and sit with her at the meeting table, the same Russian adviser entered, again without asking for permission, to ask for a document.

He said, "Comrade Anahita, where is that letter?" She replied that it was somewhere on her office desk, and the Russian adviser ignored all mannerisms or official protocols, going behind her desk to search for the letter. He opened and closed her private drawers until he found what he was looking for.

Then, without thanking or bidding the minister farewell, he left the office. That was the second blow to my head.

While I was sitting with the minister, a telephone call came from the head of the third political division in Istiqlal High School. The person on the phone said to the minister, "Comrade Anahita, I nominated one person as the President of Physical Education, and you have appointed someone else. What is the reason behind this?"

The minister replied, "Dear Comrade, those times have passed. Now, we can't put our steps forward without the permission of our Russian comrades. The Russian advisor has directly nominated the person to me," and the conversation ended.

To make matters worse, I met a Tajiki Persian translator who I knew from the planning office after leaving the minister's office. He asked me about my whereabouts and mentioned that he had not seen me for quite some time in the planning office. I told him that I had been reassigned to the construction unit, to which he immediately nodded, detailing how they had approved my assignment. That was the third blow to my head since everyone knew me, from President Babrak Karmal down to Dr . Anahita, but they still needed the Russians' permission for my reappointment. An extreme feeling of subservience had started to engulf me.

In October 1980, I received a letter from the Ministry of Planning asking for an updated and detailed progress report for constructing schools in the country. As soon received, the letter responded with some factual information to the Minister of Planning, mentioning that Mujahideen had destroyed most of the schools; Moreover, in most provinces, the money for school construction had been robbed from the banks by the so-called Mujahideen. Roads are also closed, and nobody would dare go to the site of schools. Therefore, how could I give a progress report? I sent copies of the same letter to the Minister of Education and the Minister of Finance.

When the Minister of Finance and his Russian adviser read my response and found that I had exposed the facts about the country, they got nervous. The Minister of Finance called me and said that a Russian adviser would come to meet me. Russian adviser from the Ministry of Finance came to my office and inquired about my letter addressed to the Ministry of Planning and Finance. He wanted to know who had written this letter so he could kill him.

Infuriated, I thumped the table with my fist and said that the Finance Minister told me he was sending me an adviser and not an executioner. Unable to withstand another blow that day, I got up from the meeting and left the room to return to my office.

After reality had wholly sunk in, I told myself that this country was not mine anymore. Though I had already applied for a position in the World Bank, the Russian adviser's death threat made me realize that I had to leave the country with my family as soon as possible while my dignity and honour remained intact.

I had to do something for the freedom of my beloved motherland Afghanistan, but from outside rather than inside. Unfortunately, however, the next day, I had to be admitted to a hospital because of a heart attack, where I spent the next four months. Fear of my death and the pain of seeing my country losing its sovereignty had been too much to bear, to stay in my beloved motherland Afghanistan, and do nothing.

Nevertheless, it was evident that choosing between warfare or a peaceful approach was paramount to ending my Afghan nation from imposed inhuman political crises and disasters. Thus selecting either one of them strongly affects the settlement of the issue.

Therefore, people whose nation is facing imposed crises, disasters, and atrocities must be willing to find a solution to achieve the aim of peace and end the crises. The people have to choose between obtaining this goal through a violent struggle or a nonviolent approach.

I am sure that all peace-loving people will agree that the perpetuation of war is not humane for ending such a crisis in a nation. Therefore, we all prefer to solve the imposed war through a dignified and peaceful approach.

I am also a man who has never even handled an air gun. I am someone who hates violence and its perpetrators by nature. I chose the peaceful approach as my direction for everything in life, mainly to serve the needful welfare of my beloved Afghan nation. But after my beloved motherland, Afghanistan was invaded by the Red Army of the Soviet Union, I lost all my hopes.

Since then, whether I was in or out of my beloved country, conscientiously been under pressure and mentally disturbed by the unbearable state of affairs in Afghanistan. Hence, to save my Afghan nation from bloodshed, further disaster, and destruction, I have always supported finding a dignified political and peaceful settlement of the Afghanistan issue.

Therefore, my consideration and motive in writing the following letters with some proposals in last 44 years were to open myself without hesitation in approaching the soul and minds of the world leaders, including the political parties in Afghanistan, Iran, and Pakistan, the secretary-general of the United Nations, the chairperson of the nonaligned conference, the secretary-general of the Islamic conference, and all the peace-loving people of the world, and all my Afghan brothers and sisters.

We ought to, as human beings and defenders of human rights, join our hands together to find a diplomatic solution to the Afghanistan issue and a solution to build an enduring peace and restore freedoms, national sovereignty, and territorial integrity of my motherland Afghanistan. Without peace in Afghanistan, global peace will be but a distant dream.

Thus, to achieve my goal, in March 1981, I managed to get out of Afghanistan with my family and go to Bombay (present-day Mumbai), India, as council general of Afghanistan.

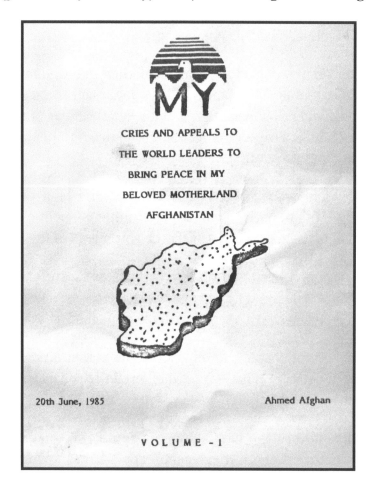

On October 2, 1984, I disseminated my first letter to the secretary-general of the United Nations and the world leaders. Later, on June 20, 1985, I released my first six letters in a booklet titled My Cries and Appeals to the World Leaders to Bring Peace in My Beloved Motherland, Afghanistan.

Since then, I have continued to write letters, proposals, hundreds of articles, and several books to express my views and bring to readers' attention the ongoing heart-wrenching atrocities in Afghanistan. Through my writings, I urge my Afghan fellow citizens and world leaders to strive for peace and restoration of freedom, national unity, sovereignty, and territorial integrity of Afghanistan.

Here in this chapter, which is under the title of "The Cries and appeals of Afghan," I am sure that in the end, kind readers will come to conclude that the atrocities in the last thirty-seven years, beginning April 27, 1978, in Afghanistan, are the undeniable collaboration of the internal and external conspirators.

Last but not least, I would like to admit because of my personal and my family security during my tenure as Consul General and my stay in India, I chose to have a pen name (Ahmed Afghan) without my mailing address in my letters. So, I posted all my letters in one package to Arif Djalili son of my sister-in-law in France to mail them to the individual addresses I had already written on the envelopes. So, I am grateful to Mr. Arif Djalili and thank him from the bottom of my heart. The letters and proposals in this book titled "THE CRIES AND APPEALS OF AFGHAN" from August 1984 to 21/02/2021 are my genuine appeals to many world leaders, organizations and individuals, written in my third language over a long period. I have tried to keep them in their original form in this book. However, if there are minor changes in the format or noticing some English mistakes, I humbly apologize.

I hope the reader will better understand the depth of my anguish and my persistently, ever-hopeful longing for the peace and prosperity of my beloved motherland, Afghanistan.

Thank God despite all my health problems and economical burdens for allowing me to reflect on my cries and appeals from 1885 to 21/02/2021 to reach the heart and minds of readers In these books, Conferences, emails, and hundreds of articles on different websites and Facebook.

LETTERS AND PROPOSALS SENT FROM MUMBAI (BOMBAY) INDIA

LETTER I

August 2, 1984

Mr. Javier Pérez de Cuellar
United Nations Secretary-General
United Nations Organization
866 United Nations Plaza
New York, NY 10017
USA

Your Excellency,

It is a great honour and pleasure for me to convey my heartiest congratulations and good wishes for Your Excellency's efforts and endeavours to bring about peace in the world.

Your Excellency's efforts towards finding a prestigious solution for the political settlement of the Afghanistan issue are also muchly appreciable to the absolute majority of the people of Afghanistan, the people of the South Asian region, and all peace-loving people of the world.

It is sad that due to the stubbornness of the two superpowers and the selfishness, needless competition and ideological differences of some of the leaders of tiny groups of my Afghan brothers and sisters. They are organized into different parties and forced to disagree with a peaceful approach to the political settlement of the Afghanistan issue. The kind and humane efforts of the United Nations Assembly, conferences of the nonaligned countries, and of the Islamic countries, and even the personal initiatives and efforts of Your Excellency as a General Secretary of the United Nations towards the Political Settlement of the Afghanistan issue have not yielded any positive result. The two superpowers will never agree on the Political Settlement of Afghanistan issue till they have succeeded in imposing their will on the people of Afghanistan and achieving their perfidious aims in Afghanistan and thereby in the South Asian region.

Therefore, I have to say that there is no hope of any political settlement of the Afghanistan issue under the United Nations-sponsored indirect talks in Geneva, beginning on August 24, 1984, unless Your Excellency takes some concrete steps and actions. We Afghans want your influence to be used on the two superpowers to agree on the political settlement of the Afghanistan issue as soon as possible.

Otherwise, not only will the inhuman crisis continue in Afghanistan, but it will also jeopardize the peace in the South Asian region. It is a fact that the majority of the Afghans will never forget their proud history; the two superpowers should realize that the Afghans have an account of taking whatever is theirs by right, through struggle, since they were born amidst their sacrifices in wars and battles.

As such, they are not the people to plead for concessions and forget the proud historical heritage of their forefathers. All the Afghan will struggle and fight for their freedom, independence and national sovereignty till the last breath of the last Afghan. There is a question, why are the people of Afghanistan being misused and sacrificed by the stubbornness of the so-called defenders of human rights, namely, the two superpowers? Suppose the two superpowers are honest and faithful human rights defenders and are willing to bring an acceptable and prestigious peace, freedom, independence and national sovereignty to Afghanistan.

In that case, they should join hands with the United Nations-sponsored mission for the prestigious political settlement of the Afghanistan issue to achieve this sacred and genuine desire.

As an Afghan and a servant of the patriotic people of my dear beloved motherland Afghanistan, I give courage to myself and strongly urge, appeal, cry and humbly request Mr. Ronald Reagan, President of the United States of America, Mr. Konstantin Chernenko, General Secretary of the Communist Party, the President of the Soviet Union, General Zia-ul-Haq, President of Pakistan,Imam Ayatollah Khomeini, the revolutionary leader of the Islamic Republic of Iran, the leader of the People's Republic of China, Mrs. Indira Gandhi, Prime Minister of the Republic of India and Chairperson of the Non-Aligned Movement, the General Secretary of the Islamic Conferences, all other leaders and peoples of the world, my Afghan freedom fighters refugee brothers and sisters, as well as brothers and sisters of the People's Democratic, Afghan Milat, Masawat, Sitam-a-Mili, National Unity, Sholee-Javed, and all Islamic parties of Afghanistan and all my revolutionary patriotic countryman living in Afghanistan and abroad to come together for forgive and forget their differences, disputes, disparity, competition, egotism, hatred, revenge, cruelty, hate, expansionism, hegemonism, exploitation for the sake of Allah, the Holiest of Holies, for the sake of those bridegrooms who lost their brides, brides who lost their bridegrooms, fathers who have lost their kith and kin and innocent young sons and these children have lost their beloved guardians, ladies who have lost their dearest husbands, brothers, sisters, and those brothers and sisters who have lost their legs, arms, nose, ears, eyes, minds, and conscience.

For the sake of those who have lost their dearest relatives, friends, shelters, and orphans who have nobody to look after them.
For the sake of refugees have been living in unbearable conditions abroad.
For the sake of those tortured in prisons and mentally disturbed and embarrassed by looking at their wounds?
For the sake of those wounded whose wounds have not yet healed up, the injured people in the deserts and mountains are losing their lives for a sip of water.
For the sake of those Afghans martyred in deserts and mountains, whose flesh has been eaten by merciless vultures, or those buried alive or who have lost their lives in prison.

For the sake of all, my Afghan brothers and sisters have been suffering from depression and disappointment.

For the sake of those innocent Afghans hanged up in prisons or buried in mass graves.

For the sake of those drowned in the rivers and their flesh being eaten by fish and other animals.

For the sake of those who have been pushed down from the Airplanes, their bodies have been eaten by wild animals and birds.

For the sake of those killed inhumanly by chemicals, even the birds and animals died by eating their flesh.

For the sake of those who have suffocated and lost their lives in the underground gulley.

For the sake of those mothers and fathers are still crying and impatiently waiting for their martyred sons and losing their eyesight.

For the sake of those who have been ripped off into pieces due to the blasts of bombs and other evil events that happened in my dear motherland Afghanistan since April 27, 1978.

Finally, for the success of the coming United Nations-sponsored indirect talks in Geneva to stop suffocation, crisis, disasters, afflictions and massacres in Afghanistan, and bring national reconciliation to restore peace, unity, integrity, solidarity, brotherhood, friendship, harmony, independence, national sovereignty, nonalignment and rehabilitation of Afghanistan with a desire established a National Progressive Democratic Republic Government in Afghanistan, and a genuine desire to build a new blossomed and splendid Afghanistan for the noble, kind, patriotic, robust, brave, proud, manly, generous, well-built, stalwart, virile, steadfast, potent, gallant, warlike, brave, warriors, hospitable and peace-loving people of Afghanistan.

It is also a great privilege and honour for me to draw your kind attention to my proposals enclosed for the political settlement of the Afghanistan issue. I hope some of the points will be useful in future talks and a copy of this letter. Finally, I approach with a request to the involved and concerned leaders and parties for their urgent, kind, genuine, loyal, sympathetic, positive, and humane action towards the prestigious political settlement of the Afghanistan issue. I avail of this opportunity to renew my appeal to Your Excellency and assure you of my highest confederation.

God bless you.

Yours truly,
Ahmed Afghan

CC:

Mr. Ronald Reagan, President of the United States of America

Mr. Konstantin Chernenko, General Secretary of Communist Party and Presidium of the USSR

General Zia-UL-Huq, President of the Republic of Pakistan Islamabad, Pakistan

Imam Ayatollah Khomeini, Revolutionary leader of the Islamic Republic of Iran, Tehran, Iran

Mrs. Indira Gandhi, Prime Minister of Republic of India and Chairperson of Non-Aligned Conference, Minister of Foreign Affairs, New Delhi, India

The Leader of the People's Republic of China, Peking, China

Mr. Habib Shati, General Secretary of PDPA and the President of the Revolutionary Council of the Democratic Republic of Afghanistan

A PROPOSAL FOR THE PRESTIGIOUS POLITICAL SETTLEMENT OF THE AFGHANISTAN ISSUE

A. MAIN PRINCIPLES:

A.1. Political recognition of the Democratic Republic of Afghanistan as a transitory government for a period of continuous fifteen-month by those governments who have recognized the Republic of Afghanistan before April 27, 1978, to start direct talks between the transitory Government of Afghanistan and Governments of the Republic of Pakistan, Islamic Republic of Iran, and the Representative of a United body of all the Afghan refugees, under the auspices of the United Nations to reach a positive and a generally acceptable prestigious political settlement of the Afghanistan issue, based on the following items.

A.2. Non-interference of the other states in the internal and external affairs of Afghanistan, mainly by the Governments of the Republic of Pakistan, Islamic Republic of Iran, Republic of India, People's Republic of China, the Soviet Union, and the United States of America.

A.3. The prestigious and honourable gradual return of all the Afghan refugees from the soil of Pakistan and Iran to Afghanistan with the simultaneous smooth and gradual recovery of all the Soviet troops from Afghanistan to the Soviet Union in the twelve-month continuously as mentioned in the implementation program of the plan of operation for the political settlement of the Afghanistan issue.

A.4. Establishing a new Parliamentary System under the name of NATIONAL PROGRESSIVE DEMOCRATIC REPUBLIC OF AFGHANISTAN (MADRAS), which will comprise educated, intellectual, progressive and authorized members who are elected freely & fairly of the people's Democratic, United Islamic, Shola- e-Javed, Afghan Milat, Massawat, Sitam-e-Milli, National Unity and other recognized parties in Afghanistan.

A.5. Recognizing Islam as a sacred state religion, respecting the national traditions, cultures, languages, and different sects and other religious groups in Afghanistan.

A.6. Maintaining national independence with national sovereignty, territorial sovereignty, national integration, national benefits, non-interference of religion, language and other sects in the political affairs, and also active and positive nonalignment, freedom of judgment in internal and international affairs, respect for the united nations charter, mutual friendship, and respect for the neighbouring as well as Islamic countries, and all other peace-loving nations of the world.

- To reorganize the national life in Afghanistan according to the requirements of the time and based on the realities of national history and culture.
- To achieve justice, equality and legality in all sections of Afghanistan.
- Organize the functions of the state and its branches to ensure all democratic, political, and social liberties and the welfare of all the individuals in the sections of Afghanistan.
- To achieve all individual and social security in all sections of Afghanistan.
- To achieve a balanced development of all phases of life in Afghanistan.
- Organize the functions of the state and its branches to ensure the speedy rehabilitation of Afghanistan.
- To form, ultimately, a prosperous and progressive society based on social cooperation and preservation of dignity & honour.

A.7. Agreement of all the concerned parties, particularly the transitory Government of Afghanistan and the Governments of Pakistan, Iran, Soviet Union, China and the United States of America, on enforcement of the implementation programme of the plan of operation for the political settlement of Afghanistan issue by an International Monitoring Team.

A.8. Approval of the Security Council, particularly of all its permanent members of the Security Council of the United Nations on the Main Principles for the political settlement and the implementation programme of the plan of operation for the political settlement of the Afghanistan issue.

B. IMPLEMENTATION PROGRAMME OF THE PLAN OF OPERATION

B.1. - FIRST PHASE (THREE CONTINUOUS MONTHS)

B.1.1 - Establishment of international centers under the direct control of the sponsored missions of the United Nations to create a Special Relief Fund for the return and settlement of the Afghan refugees into their respective native places for the overall rehabilitation of Afghanistan.

B.1.2 - Finding the total number of Afghan refugees by distinguishing men, women and children in Pakistan and Iran by the United Nations mission through collaborative efforts of the hosting countries of the refugees and the authorized representatives of the refugees in these countries.

B.1.3 - Geographically distributing Afghanistan into six regions on the Afghanistan map and finding the number of Afghan refugees in each region stationed in Pakistan and Iran by the mission appointed by the United Nations.

B.1.4 - Presenting the actual number of the Soviet troops, including captains, commanders, and all military advisers, stationed in Afghanistan by the said mission of the United Nations.

B.1.5 - Finding the ratio of the Soviet troops in Afghanistan and the Afghan refugees on the soils of Pakistan and Iran based on the information of items no. B 12, B 13, B 14, by the Joint Mission of the transitory Government of Afghanistan and the Government of Republic of Pakistan and the Islamic Republic of Iran under the defect collaboration of the United Nations missions for the political settlement of Afghanistan issue.

B.1.6 - Appointing a joint mission, including the representative of the transitory Government of Afghanistan, to fix the type and amount of the relief fund and the distribution of international relief funds for the Afghan refugees after their return to their respective native places in Afghanistan.

B.1.7 - Providing and furnishing information regarding the actual number of Afghan refugees by the other hosting countries in their receptive countries and arrangements for their prestigious return to Afghanistan, presenting the same to the mission appointed by the United Nations.

B.1.8 - Fixing the schedule and programme for the return and disarmament of the refugees of each region in six different stages according to the number of refugees in each area and simultaneous return of The Soviet troops to the Soviet Union in proportion to the number of Afghan refugees returned to each region

B.2. - SECOND PHASE (TWELVE CONTINUOUS MONTHS)

B.2.1 - Declaration of the schedule and programme of the gradual return and disarmament of the Afghan refugees from Pakistan and Iran to Afghanistan according to the fixed regions in six different stages during the twelve continuous months, followed by the declaration of the schedule and programme of the simultaneous gradual return of the Soviet troops to the Soviet Union from Afghanistan.

B.2.2 - Commencement of the gradual return of all the Afghan refugees and the simultaneous gradual recovery of the Soviet troops to the Soviet Union according to the programme, as mentioned in item Nos. B.1.5, B.1.6, of phase one, and item no. B.1.2 in phase two.

B.2.3 - Blocking the returned refugees of each region by the United Nations Peacekeeping force till the end of the gradual return of all the Afghan refugees to their native places in Afghanistan and the simultaneously gradual return of all Soviet troops to the Soviet Union.

B.2.4 - Blocking the routes of the refugees to Pakistan and Iran by the United Nations Peacekeeping force till the final return of all the refugees.

B.2.5 - Declaration of a program for returning Afghan refugees from other countries to Afghanistan according to the program fixed in item no. B.1.7 in phase one.

B.2.6 - Releasing all the prisoners who have been imprisoned since April 27, 1978.

B.2.7 - Declaring the "WINDING UP" of the program and successful implementation of the schedule and plan for the gradual return of all the Afghan refugees to Afghanistan and a simultaneously gradual return of all the Soviet troops, commanders, captains and military advisers to their country.

B.3. - THIRD PHASE (FIVE CONTINUOUS MONTHS)

B.3.1 - Dissolution of the transitory Government of Afghanistan and declaration of national reconciliation, harmony, solidarity and integrity in Afghanistan.

B.3.2 - Establishing an INTERIM NATIONAL MULTI-PARTY COUNCIL (INMPC) made of leaders and the authorized representative of each party mentioned in items nos. A.4, A.5, A.6, A.7, A.8, with a chairperson belonging to a neutral body which would be acceptable to all members of (INMPC).

B.3.3 - Assigning an absolute neutral, immaculate, loyal, patriotic Prime Minister by (INMPC) who will be capable and acceptable to all the members of the cabinet for forming the Interim Government in which all the cabinet members will consist of the nominees of the parties mentioned in item nos. A4, A5, A6, A7, A8.

B.3.4 - Appointing a Committee by NMPC under the direct Chairmanship of the Prime Minister to prepare the new constitution according to the instructions given in item No. A 4.

B.3.5 - Holding a free and fair national election for the Grand National Assembly throughout the country under the direct supervision and control of the Interim Government and the International Monitoring Team for the Grand National Assembly, which would be convened in the city of Kabul for sanctioning the new constitution.

B.3.6 - Declaring the sanctioning of the new constitution of the NATIONAL PROGRESSIVE DEMOCRATIC DEMOCRATIC REPUBLIC OF AFGHANISTAN and holding free and fair national elections for the Parliament, and inauguration of the Parliament by the President of the Interim National Multi-party Council to elect a new President and members of the First National Multi-Party Council from amongst the elected member of the Parliament. A new Prime Minister of the National Progressive Democratic Republic of Afghanistan should also be appointed by NMPC, and they must introduce the Prime Minister for acceptance to the National Multi-Party Parliament and, after that, announce the political settlement of the Afghanistan issue and thereby commencing new life in Afghanistan.

- Ahmed Afghan

P.S. CONSPIRACIES AND ATROCITIES IN AFGHANISTAN

* The People's Democratic (Khalq & Parcham), Afghan Milat, Massawat, Sitam-e-milli, Shola-e-Java and Islamic were the only established parties in Afghanistan according to the constitution of 1964. These were known and active up to 1973, after which their activities went underground till the People's Democratic Party took power on April 27, 1978.

LETTER II

September 10, 1984

Mr. Javier Pérez de Cuellar
United Nations Secretary-General United Nations Organization United Nations Plaza
866 United Nations Plaza
New York, NY 10017
USA

Your Excellency,

I have the honoured state that appears to be the follow-up of my letters of August 2, 1984, which I feel Your Excellency must have received before the 3rd round of indirect talks on the Political Settlement of Afghanistan issue in Geneva. A copy of my previous letters addressed to Your Excellency is herewith attached.

As mentioned in my previous letter, the talks did not yield a positive solution. Therefore, according to my speculation, the superpowers, for reaching their perfidious aims once again, got some time for the massacre and making the innocent and poor people of Afghanistan fight and ultimately kill each other.

I am sure that the fourth round of indirect talks, after a lapse of six months, will be the same as the last three rounds. One of the reasons is the non-unity among the refugee brothers and sisters for introducing their one representative to the United Nations to participate in the United Nations indirect talks sponsored by the United Nations.

The other reason is that the Soviet Union was not prepared to give the schedule for the withdrawal of their troops, and they weren't interested in committing the departure of their forces from Afghanistan.

Therefore once again, I request all brothers and sisters humbly belonging to all known political parties, heroic military brothers and sisters, all the civilian brothers and sisters, and all my patriotic fellow citizens living in Afghanistan and abroad to give up their differences & individual struggle and killing each other for power and foreign ideologies such as socialism, imperialism and so on. I would therefore appeal to my brothers and sisters to tread the path of our Afghan ancestors and be united to form a strong, solid, iron force against the natural foreign enemies to get freedom, independence, national sovereignty and peaceful life.

We must strive hard to establish the federal regressive democratic Republic Government in Afghanistan. I also request the refugee brothers and sisters to introduce themselves as one united body to the United Nations and introduce one representative to the United Nations to join the Mission of Political Settlement of the Afghanistan issue under the sponsorship of the United Nations.

May I humbly request Your Excellency to explain and give an accurate picture of the happenings of events in Afghanistan and provide a summary of the three rounds of the indirect talks to the members of the coming General Assembly? This would allow them to make some reasonable and practical decisions regarding the prestigious political settlement of the Afghanistan issue.

Could I also request Your Excellency to emphasize some positive and urgent steps, please, while using your good influence on the leaders of the Soviet Union, the United States of America and other powers involved in the Afghanistan issue, to achieve a mutual agreement for the prestigious political settlement of the Afghanistan issue?

I would also request Your Excellency to please not mix and link the Afghanistan issue with the general political situation of the world. If the matter is connected with the prevailing situation, the Afghanistan problem will never be solved.

Kindly do the needful to find the right solution to expedite the issue to bring peace, freedom, independence, national sovereignty, territorial sovereignty and non-aligned status to Afghanistan as soon as possible. Otherwise, the foreign enemies of Afghanistan will bring the war beyond the borders of Afghanistan and thereby create a new problem by which Afghanistan will lose its identity and its freedom, independence and national sovereignty and territorial sovereignty forever.

I avail of this opportunity to give Your Excellency the assurances of my highest consideration.

God bless you.

Yours truly,
Ahmed Afghan

CC:
Mr. Diego Cordovez, UNO
Mr. Konstantin Chernenko, Leader of USSR
Mrs. Indira Gandhi, Chairperson of Non-Aligned Movement, Prime Minister of India
HE General Zia-ul-Haq, Leader of the Government of Pakistan
Imam Ayatollah Khomeini, Leader of the Islamic Republic of Iran
HE President of Yugoslavia
HE President of Sri Lanka, Mr. Jayawardene
Mr. Babrak Karmal, President of the Revolutionary Council and General-Secretary of the People's Democratic Party of Afghanistan
Mr. Ronald Reagan, President of the United States of America
Mr. General Wojciech Jaruselski, Leader and Prime Minister of Poland

LETTER III

December 31, 1984

Shri Rajeev Gandhi
Prime Minister of India
Minister of Foreign Affairs
New Delhi

Your Excellency,

I take this opportunity to offer my hearty congratulations to Your Excellency on your unanimous victory as Prime Minister of the Great Indian Republic.

The integrity and solidarity of India during the elections prove that a lot of confidence is reposed in Your Excellency from the people of India. I am sure there are many other problems and tasks before you, and shortly you will be busy solving the internal and external affairs concerning India, and particularly the significant, exciting issues of the world as your good self-being as Chairperson of the Non-Aligned Movement.

Let me express myself mostly humbly by saying that in this critical condition of the world, mainly when the crises are happening in Afghanistan. Not only do the Indian brothers and sisters have high expectations from Your Excellency, but also your millions of Afghan brothers and sisters who are suffering from the miseries, calamities, and distress during the last five years due to the open Soviet military invasion of Afghanistan on December 27, 1979, resulting in the brutal killing of hundreds of thousands of innocent children, youngsters and older people. It destroyed their properties and forced millions of people to run away from their beloved motherland, making them refugees who are now living in challenging conditions in different countries as they have lost their national sovereignty, territorial sovereignty, freedom, independence and nonalignment. They are waiting and looking forward very anxiously to Your Excellency's urgent humanitarian action.

At this juncture, as you have been unanimously elected as a prominent young, dynamic, hardworking and respected leader of the great Indian Republic, and being the Chairperson of the Non-Aligned Movement, I, as an Afghan brother of yours, request Your Excellency to take strong, positive and independent steps. Urge you to use the power and influence of your good self to convince the leaders of the USSR and the USA to reach a mutual agreement to solve the Afghanistan issue and thereby end the crisis, resulting in granting the right to the people of Afghanistan to establish a National Progressive Democratic Republic by themselves for own selves and bring back peace, national sovereignty, freedom, independence and the non-aligned status of Afghanistan to concurrently bring about peace in the South Asian region, thus solving the present tensions of the world.

I have already forwarded my proposals to bring about peace in my beloved country Afghanistan, enclosed in my letters of August 2, 1984. September 10, 1984, addressed to his Excellency Mr. Javier Perez de Cuellar, the General Secretary of the United Nations and sent copies to your great and beloved mother, late Mrs. Indira Gandhi, the Champion of Peace, Prime Minister of India and Chairperson of the Non-Aligned Movement.

Therefore, for your kind information and knowledge, I request Your Excellency to personally go through the proposals and take strong, positive and urgent steps towards the prestigious political settlement of the Afghanistan issue.

Copies for your kind perusal and record are enclosed.
I take this opportunity to assure Your Excellency of my highest consideration.

God bless you.

Yours truly,
Ahmed Afghan

CC:
His Excellency Mr. Javier Perez de Cuellar, The Secretary General,
United Nations, 866, United Nations Plaza, New York, NY 10017, USA

LETTER IV

January 24, 1985

HE Mr. Syed Sharifuddin Peerzadah,
General Secretary for Islamic Conference
Jeddah
Saudi Arabia

Your Excellency,

It is my pleasure and honour to congratulate you on your election as General Secretary of the Islamic Conference. I wish you all the best and grand success in all walks of your dynamic personality.

I know you will face many crucial problems in your new assignment, facing present critical conditions of the world and finding an immediate solution for each of these problems. But, I'm here to speak to you as an Afghan who has been seeing and seriously observing the severe crises in my dear beloved motherland of Afghanistan since April 1978, particularly after the open military invasion of the Soviet Union on December 27, 1979.

It has resulted in the brutal killing of innocent people, destroying their property, torturing them, putting them in prison without any reason and forcing them to leave their beloved country and live in unbearable rather miserable conditions. Therefore, I consider this one of the most crucial and immediate problems to be given priority in Your Excellency's tasks.

Since you are not biased by the policies of either of the two powers, instead you are willing very sincerely to act like a man of peace, enthusiastically interested in preserving and maintaining stability in the region, and thereby in the world; I would humbly request Your Excellency to kindly take immediate, strong and positive action on humanitarian ground and to find the solution for the Afghanistan issue as soon as possible.

This is because the Soviet Union and the United States of America have their eyes on achieving their hegemony and colonial aims in the region and the world and trying their utmost to create hurdles for aborting the indirect talks in connection with the political settlement of the Afghanistan issue to be held in Geneva under the auspices of the United Nations, under such circumstances for the last few months the Government of the Democratic Republic of Afghanistan is compelled to accuse the Governments of Pakistan and Iran for their aggression.

Likewise, Pakistan and Iran are also accusing Afghanistan in the same manner; thereby, they are indirectly expressing their unwillingness to continue the indirect talk and trying to make the 4th round of indirect negotiations for a political settlement of the Afghanistan issue more challenging and unlikely to be held next February, as was scheduled during the 3rd round of indirect talks in Geneva.

There is doubt that the Soviet Union is trying to considerably increase its military ties and force in Afghanistan in the immediate future to seal off the so-called borders of Afghanistan and Pakistan, the boundaries of Afghanistan with Iran, and ultimately isolate Afghanistan from the rest of the world.

This will result in Afghanistan just maintaining its flag and representation in the United Nations, like the Republic of Ukraine of the Soviet Union and being called an independent country.

But, still, in reality, it would be the 16th Republic of the Soviet Union with no freedom, independence, national sovereignty, territorial sovereignty and nonalignment status forever.

After having it under its complete and direct domination, it is then swallowing all the new natural resources of Afghanistan and using the soil of Afghanistan as a platform for the next jump to Pakistan, India, the Indian Ocean and the Persian Gulf.

But, on the other hand, the United States of America, on the pretext of maintaining peace in the region and defending the rights of Afghans, fighting the Soviet Union to the last Afghan, is trying to change the soil of Pakistan as their Military base against Soviet Union Afghanistan, Pakistan, India, Iran Indian Ocean & Persian Gulf, as a result of the actions of the superpowers, the poor, innocent, peace-loving people of Afghanistan, Pakistan, India and Iran would suffer. It would have to pay the price now and in future.

Therefore, once again, I humbly suggest the following proposal to Your Excellency for the cause of the prestigious political settlement of the Afghanistan issue to maintain peace in the South Asian region and the world.

1. Please call upon a joint mission talks with His Excellency Mr. Javier Perez Culler, General Secretary of the United Nations, His Excellency Mr. Raheev Gandhi, the Prime Minister of India and the Chairperson of the Non-Aligned Movement, to discuss the crises of Afghanistan and take some concrete positive decisions to achieve the solution for the prestigious political settlement of Afghanistan issue.

2. The decision arrived at the joint mission to be forwarded to the so-called human rights, Mr. Ronald Reagan, President of The United States of America and Mr. Konstantin Cherneko, Leader of the Soviet Union.

3. Once this agreement has been achieved, a summit Conference of the authorized representative of the government of the Soviet Union, United States of America, China, Afghanistan, Pakistan, and Iran and an acceptable elected representative of all Afghani refugees who are settled either in Pakistan, Iran and other parts of the world, be called in Geneva under auspices of H. E. Mr. Javier Perez de Cuellar, General Secretary of the United Nations, H.E. Mr. Rajiv Gandhi, Chairperson of the Non-Aligned Movement and Your Excellency General Secretary of Islamic

Conference. You are requested to go through the proposal and agree upon the decision to forward it by ratifying it for approval by the United Nations.

4. One of the obstacles regarding the indirect talks on the prestigious political settlement of Afghanistan issue under the auspices of the United Nations has unfortunately not yielded a final positive solution. Due to the non-unity amongst the Afghan refugees in Pakistan, Iran and other parts of the world. The apparent reason for their not being united is that the enemies are still using the policy of divide and rule among the Afghan refugees.

The latter has been segregated into many groups under different names with different Leaders, and each group is connected to another financial supporter who has been obliged to follow their instructions. Failing to do so would result in them losing their privileges.

I would therefore like to express by saying that if the same prevailing conditions dominate the Afghan refugees, there will be no unity amongst the refugees against their common enemies for the cause of restoring peace, freedom, independence, national sovereignty, territorial sovereignty and non-aligned status of their beloved motherland Afghanistan and hence all financial assistance from different sources would not only be helpful to solve the problem of Afghanistan but, the bloodshed and crises will drag on till the last Afghan.

Then, finally, the Soviet Union would win the battle and reach the Indian Ocean and the Persian Gulf.

In connection with the unity of all the different leaders of the Afghan refugees, I would like to request Your Excellency to take the initiative to solve this significant problem as soon as possible. I am also forwarding the following points to Your Excellency as my personal views for the cause of the unity of all my brave revolutionary refugee brothers and sisters.

An a. The humanitarian help and assistance of the Government of Pakistan, Iran, Islamic countries and all other peace-loving nations should be brought under one umbrella.

b. All financial organizations should join and form a Coordination Committee in one center for collecting donations and assistance on a humanitarian basis.

c. All humanitarian financial assistance thus collected should be distributed directly under the supervision of the representatives of the Coordination Committee to all the brave.

d. The leaders of different groups of all the Afghan revolutionary refugees stationed either in Pakistan, Iran, or other parts of the world and the representatives of the governments of Pakistan and Iran be called to the Coordination Center to discuss the essentials of unity of different leaders of Afghan refugees for the cause of encouraging the financial sources for getting the humanitarian assistance required for meeting their needs and the distribution to all Afghan refugees by proper and fastest means the ways.

e. After achieving unity amongst different leaders of the refugees only, one person as a leader for all the refugees be elected and introduced to the Coordination Committee as a contact person with the responsibility of all financial matters as a single leader in the summit conference mentioned in item no.2 and the same person could be at the indirect talks on a prestigious political settlement of Afghanistan issue, by the United Nations.

After achieving a concrete and positive proposal for the prestigious political settlement of the Afghanistan issue, it would result in the simultaneous smooth withdrawal of all Soviet Union Military forces from the soil of Afghanistan and dignified return of all Afghan refugees from the ground of Pakistan, Iran and the other parts of the world. It would thereby restore peace, freedom, national sovereignty, territorial sovereignty and the non-aligned state of Afghanistan.

Your Excellency as General Secretary of the Islamic Conference, His Excellency Mr. Javier Perez de Cuellar, General Secretary to the United Nations and His Excellency Mr. Rajeev Gandhi, Chairperson of the Non-Aligned Movement, unitedly will make an invaluable contribution to the cause of preservation of peace in the region and ultimately in the world.

By the way, I would also like to refer to the enclosed copies of my letters and proposals for the political settlement of the Afghanistan issue dated August 2, 1984, along with letters dated September 10, 1984, addressed to His Excellency Mr. Javier Perez de Cuellar, General Secretary of the United Nations and the letter dated December 31, 1984, addressed to His Excellency Mr. Rejeev Gandhi, Prime Minister of India and the Chairperson of the Non-Aligned Movement, for your perusal.

I avail of this opportunity to give Your Excellency the assurances of my highest consideration.

God bless you.

Yours truly
Ahmed Afghan

cc:
His Excellency MrJavier Perez de Cuellar, General Secretary of the United Nations.
His Excellency Mr. Rajeev Gandhi, Chairperson of the Non-Aligned Movement.
His Excellency Imam Ayatollah Khomeini, Leader of the Islamic Republic of Iran.
His Excellency General Zia-ul-Haq, Leader of the Republic of Pakistan.

LETTER V

March 14, 1985

Mr. Mikhail Gorbachev,
Secretary of the Communist Party
Soviet Union, Moscow
USSR

Your Excellency,

I have a great honour to express that your election as General Secretary of the Communist Party of the Soviet Union (CPSU) at this critical condition of the world opens a new horizon and brings new hope to the peace-loving people of the world, as the disarmament subject is dear to everyone.

Furthermore, your initiative and gestures, despite the demise of Mr. Konstantin U. Chernenko, the then leader of the Soviet Union, for the continuation of the ongoing negotiations in Geneva for arms control both on earth and in outer space are palpable and encouraging. I hope that with the cooperation of your colleague Mr. Ronald Reagan, President of the United States of America, things will move in the right direction to ensure peace in the world.

Your Excellency, I may point out that at present, the disarmament subject is not the only crucial matter in the world. There are many other vital issues in the world as well.

Therefore the people of the world have high expectations from Your Excellency, as a leader of one of the two Superpowers, to take urgent and immediate action to find the appropriate and positive solution for each of them. However, it is worth mentioning that at present, for the people of Afghanistan, Pakistan, Iran, India and all other peace-loving people of the world, the unjustifiable aggression and presence of the Soviet Union military Forces and the unbearable situation in Afghanistan are the most vital issue and should be given the top most priority in your immediate and plans and programmes.

Your Excellency, please allow me to quote part of your speech as a tribute to the late Mr. K. U. Chernenko for his efforts to half the arms race also you said, "WE AGAIN REAFFIRM THE PRINCIPLES OF GOOD NEIGHBORING RELATIONS IN PEACEFUL COOPERATION, BUT WE SAY AT THE SAME TIME THAT NO ONE WILL BE ABLE TO IMPOSE HIS WILL ON US."

In this connection, I would like to express that it could have been more appropriate by adding and saying in your speech, "WE WILL ALSO NEVER IMPOSE OUR ON OTHERS," as for the principles of good neighbourly relations and peaceful co-ope rationed in Your Excellency's speech.

I would also like to say that the people of Afghanistan, from the early days of our great and beloved king Amanullah khan and your great Leader Mr. Lenin, have established good, cordial and friendly relations between the two countries by exchanging letters dated April 7, 1919, & May 27, 1919, respectively which subsequently resulted in a treaty of the friendship of February 28, 1921, later on, a treaty of mutual non-aggression of August 31, 1926, between the two government of Afghanistan and the Soviet Union (a copy of which is enclosed for your kind perusal) ever since every five or ten years the treaty of non-aggression between the two government have had been reaffirmed of which the last one was in the year 1975.

The people of Afghanistan were faithful and loyal to the people of their great neighbour, the Soviet Union and, day by day; the economic, political and technical relations were strengthening and getting closer and closer.

But, despite the faithfulness and loyalty of the people of Afghanistan to the people of the Soviet Union, all of a sudden, without any reason, on April 27, 1978, and later on December 27, 1979, abolished all the promises and treaties between the government of the two neighbouring countries (Afghanistan & Soviet Union).

This was done by the late Mr. Breshnev, the then leader of the Soviet Union, and the same policy had been pursued by your other two predecessors, Mr. Yuri Andropov and Mr. K. U. Cherneko, resulting in the brutal killing of the innocent people of Afghanistan, destroying their houses and properties, and forcing them to leave their beloved motherland Afghanistan and live as refugees in every unbearable condition in neighbouring countries (Iran & Pakistan) and other countries of the world, leaving thousands of people handicapped and homeless.

Due to this, not only the people of Afghanistan were discontent. They lost their faithfulness and loyalty to the people of the Soviet Union. Still, internationally, the issue of the invasion of the Soviet military forces in Afghanistan has been strongly criticized by the world. It has been condemned several times by the majority of the General Assembly of the United Nations, Summit conference of the Non-Aligned Movement, Islamic meeting & other peace-loving organizations for the last six years.

Despite the initiatives which have been taken by His Excellency Mr. Javier Perez de Cuellar, General Secretary of the United Nations, to find a solution for the political Settlement of the Afghanistan issue and three rounds of indirect talks under the sponsorship of the United Nations have already been conducted between the government of the Democratic Republic of Afghanistan and the government of the Republic of Pakistan in Geneva.

But, still, unfortunately, none of them has yielded any solution because of the obstinate nature of the two superpower leaders (Soviet Union & United States of America), which badly affected the prestige of both superpowers.

Now Your election as a new leader of the Soviet Union and Warsaw Pact and as you have been praised for your benevolent nature by the leaders of the world who joined the funeral of late Mr. K. U. Chernenko brings hope to the people of Afghanistan and all the peace-loving people of the world, waiting in high expectations, looking forward to Your Excellency to take humanitarian, rightful, positive and robust initiatives jointly with your colleague, Mr. Ronald Reagan, President of the United States of America with the cooperation of His Excellency Mr. Javier Perez de Cuellar, General Secretary of the United Nations, His Excellency Mr. Peerzadah, General Secretary of Islamic Conference to end the crisis in Afghanistan with the prestigious withdrawal of all your troops from Afghanistan. I urge the refugees to be allowed to return to their beloved motherland Afghanistan from the neighbouring countries (Pakistan & Iran) and other parts of the world and restore freedom, independence, national sovereignty, territorial sovereignty and finally, the non-aligned status of Afghanistan and also for yielding my genuine desire for bringing peace in Afghanistan.

I avail this opportunity to appeal to the other six members of the Warsaw Pact to discuss the said matter very thoroughly without any fear at the Summit Conference of the Warsaw Pact scheduled to be held in Warsaw, Capital of Poland, in coming April to achieve a meaningful, positive, humanitarian division for ending the present crisis and bringing peace in Afghanistan reestablishing a new cordial and friendly relation between the people of Afghanistan with the people of Soviet Union, all socialist countries and all other Peace-loving people and countries of the World.

With a copy of this letter, I would also like to draw the kind attention of His Excellency Mr. Javier Perez de Cuellar, General, Secretary of the United Nations, His Excellency Mr. Rajive Gandhi, Chairperson of The Non-Aligned Movement, and the leaders of the six other countries of the Warsaw Pact Mr. Peerzadah, General Secretary of the Islamic Conference to join you in achieving a rightful, favourable, mutual agreement for the restoration of the prestigious peace in Afghanistan, which ultimately will bring peace in the South Asian region, and ease the tension existing in the world.

By achieving this sacred desire, not only will you take an essential humanitarian step toward peace, but it will be an act of great price for all of you.

I wish you good luck in your most courageous task; I avail this opportunity to renew to Your Excellency the assurances of my highest consideration.

God Bless You.

Yours truly
Ahmed Afghan

cc:
Mr. S. Peerzadah, General Secretary of the Islamic Conference
HE Mr. Rajive Gandhi, Prime Minister of India
HE Mr. Javier Pérez de Cuellar, General Secretary of the United Nations
HE General Jaruselski, Prime Minister of Poland
HE Mr. Todor Zhivkov, President of the People's Republic of Bulgaria
HE Mr. Gustav Husak, President of Czechoslovakia
HE Mr. Erich Honeker, General Secretary of the SED Central Committee & Chairperson of the German Democratic Republic Council
HE Mr. Nicolae Ceauşescu, President of Romania
HE Mr. O. Gostov, Present of Hungary
HE Mr. Ronald Reagan, President of the United States of America

LETTER VI

April 15, 1985

Mr. Javier Pérez de Cuellar
United Nations Secretary-General
United Nations Organization
866 United Nations Plaza
New York, NY 10017
USA

Your Excellency,

I have the honour to submit that, at present, unbearable conditions are prevailing in all parts of Afghanistan.

Therefore, over four million of its population living on the soil of Pakistan, Iran and other countries of the world, Mr. Babrak Karmal, General Secretary of the People's Democratic Party of Afghanistan and President of the revolutionary Council of the Democratic Republic of Afghanistan, has announced an unjustifiable, unacceptable and illegal election of the so-called Grand National Assembly, to talk the decision on the destiny of the innocent and unprotected people of Afghanistan against the will and consent of the absolute majority of the people, who are living in and out their home country Afghanistan.

May I assure Your Excellency that any election held or decision taken by the so-called Grand National Assembly, called by Mr. Babrak Karmal, will not only be acceptable but rejected by the absolute majority of the people of Afghanistan and all the peace-loving people of the world?

Therefore, at this critical juncture, I request Your Excellency to call an urgent extraordinary meeting of the United Nations Security Council to ratify the resolutions of the United Nations General Assembly, Non-Aligned Movement Conferences, Islamic Conference, passed on December 27, 1979. Accordingly, a solution is adopted, saying that no decision be taken by The Government of the Democratic Republic of Afghanistan under the pretext of the so-called Grand National Assembly regarding the destiny of the people of Afghanistan until a generally acceptable prestigious political settlement is achieved in connection with The Afghanistan Issue by The Sponsored Mission of the United Nations.

Once the prestigious but acceptable political settlement is reached, the transitory government in Afghanistan would declare the simultaneous smooth withdrawal of the Soviet Troops from the soil of Afghanistan and the prestigious. In honour return of all the Afghan refugees from the ground of Pakistan, Iran and other parts of the world, by restoring peace in Afghanistan, the interim government would be established to make the new constitution and hold a free and fair national election under the direct supervision and control of the United Nations for the form the Grand National Assembly to decide regarding the destiny and future of the people of Afghanistan.

With your permission, I would like to send a copy of this letter with a request to Mr. Rajiv Gandhi, the Chairperson of the Non-Aligned Movement Conferences, Mr. S. Peerzadah, General Secretary of the Islamic Conference and all other leaders of the member countries of the Security Council of the United Nations, to join hands with Your Excellency in this humanitarian and genuine desire of the people of Afghanistan.

I avail of this opportunity to give Your Excellency the assurances of my highest consideration.

God bless you.

Yours truly,
Ahmed Afghan

cc:
HE Mr. Rejiv Gandhi, Prime Minister of India and Chairperson of Non- the Aligned Conference
HE Mr. Sayed S. Peerzadah, General Secretary of the Islamic Conference
HE Mr. Ronald Regan, President of the United States of America
HE Mr. Mikhail Gorbachev, General Secretary of the Communist Party of the Soviet Union
HE Mrs. Margaret Thatcher, Prime Minister of the United Kingdom
HE Mr. Mittereand, President of France
HE Mr. Deng Xiopeng, Leader of the People's Republic of China

LETTER VII

June 4, 1985

His Excellency Mr. Rajiv Gandhi
Prime Minister of India
C/o H. E. Khurshid Alam Khan.
Minister of Foreign Affairs
New Delhi, India

Your Excellency,

I consider it a great honour to say that your Address to the Joint Session of the two houses of the United States of America on June 13, 1985, has touched me very deeply. It was excellent. Therefore, I consider it my duty to congratulate Your Excellency. I am sure your stand on the Afghanistan issue and reaffirming a political settlement that ensures the Sovereignty, Integrity, Independence and non-aligned status of Afghanistan and the return of all Afghan refugees to their homes in safety and honour is very much encouraging and appreciable to me, to the people of Afghanistan, and all the peace-loving people of the world.

I would also like to take this opportunity to thank the members of the Joint Session of the two houses of Congress for their warm welcome to Your Excellency's genuine desire for a prestigious political settlement of the Afghanistan issue.

I hope that H.E. Mr. Mikhal Gorbachov, the General Secretary of the Communist Party of the Soviet Union, will also respond positively to Your Excellency's positive and fair stand and agree on the smooth withdrawal of the Soviet troops from my dear beloved motherland Afghanistan as early as possible.

I avail of this opportunity to renew to Your Excellency the assurances of my highest consideration and thank you once again. I wish you all the success and prosperity in your future tasks.

God bless you.

Yours truly,
Ahmed Afghan

cc:
Mr. Javier Perez de Cuellar, General Secretary of United Nations
Chairman of House of Representatives, Washington DC, USA
HE Mr. Mikhail Gorbachev, General Secretary of the Communist Party of the Soviet Union, USSR
Mr. Ronald Reagan, President of the United States of America
Mr. Khurshid Alam Khan, Minister of State for Foreign Affairs of India

LETTER VIII

October 1, 1985

HE Mr. Javier Pérez de Cuellar
United Nations Secretary-General
866 United Nations Plaza
New York, NY 10017
USA

Your Excellency,

I have the honour to say that, although the consequences of the fourth and fifth round of proximity talks on the Political Settlement of Afghanistan issue have not yet achieved its final stage, it is presumed that the final decision regarding the main principles for the prestigious settlement has been suspended because of the coming summit of the two leaders of the superpowers H.E. Mr. Ronald Reagan, President of the United States of America, & H.E. Mr. Mikhall Gorbacheve, General Secretary of Communist Party of the Soviet Union, in Geneva on November, 19 & 20, 1985.

It is indeed needless to say that it has been coupled with tremendous moral force and inspiring leadership of Your Excellency, Excellent initiatives and efforts which have been taken by your representative, H.E. Mr. Deigo Gordovez in the last three years for the cause of finding a prestigious solution of the Afghanistan issue which may be acceptable to the absolute majority of the people of Afghanistan and all the peace-loving people of the world.

The demand and expectation of my humble self as an Afghan and all the peace-loving people of the World from the two leaders mentioned above in their coming summit is to prove that they are the true defenders of human rights.

Honestly, they are willing to bring peace to the world and save the world from destruction, and jointly pave the way to establish an international economic order for the cause of the prosperity of all humanity in the world.

I am sure if there is a genuine desire for peace in the coming summit of the two leaders, they will highly and sincerely consider the Political Settlement of Afghanistan issue. Constructive & decisions will be taken to smoothen the way for the success of the sixth round of talks in Geneva to be held on December 16–20, 1985, resulting in the smooth withdrawal of the Soviet Troops from Afghanistan to the Soviet Union within an acceptable schedule to all concerned parties involved and the prestigious and safe return of all the patriotic Afghan refugees from the soil of Pakistan, Iran and other parts of the World. I hope it will also lay down a firm and permanent International guarantee for peace, independence, national Sovereignty and the nonaligned status of my dear beloved motherland, Afghanistan, based on the United Nations Charter.

Once again, I take this opportunity to request your good self as General Secretary of the United Nations, H.E. Mr. Rajiv Gandhi, Prime Minister of India and Chairperson of Non-Aligned Movement, and H.E. Mr. Sayed Sharafuddin Peerzadah, General Secretary for the Islamic Conference to prevail upon the two leaders of the world to find a concrete and constructive decision on the immediate prestigious political settlement of Afghanistan issue and thereby the peace in the whole world.

It is evident that whatever decision is arrived at the coming Summit of the two leaders, it will be witnessed and recorded in the history of the world. Therefore, I pray and wish that the Summit will end without an iota of hostility and in an amicable and fraternal atmosphere, with fruitful results for the benefit and welfare of humanity and all human beings in the present and future.

I avail of this opportunity to assure Your Excellency of my highest consideration.

God bless you.

Yours truly,
Ahmed Afghan

cc:
HE Mr. Ronald Reagan, President of the USA

LETTER IX

April 17, 1986

HE Mr. Rajiv Gandhi
Prime Minister of India
C/O HE Mr. H. K. L. Bhagat
Ministry of Foreign Affairs
New Delhi, India

Your Excellency,

May I have the honour to express your inaugural address as a Chairperson of the Non-Aligned Movement to the Non-Aligned Foreign Ministers Conference held on April 16, 1986, in New Delhi, for Libya, and strongly condemning the attack of U.S. aircraft against Libya was excellent. I am sure Your Excellency's stand at this moment is appreciable to all the peace-loving nations of the world.

It was an unfortunate state of affairs when I shared my most profound grief with all my Arab brothers and sisters. I want to give courage to myself and express my deep concern against some member countries of the Non-Aligned Movement. They have yet to strongly condemn the USSR for their continuing aggression and the military invasion of Afghanistan. They haven't charged the global terrorism in the United States of America either, which has been held responsible for the latest attack on Libya.

This posture of some member countries of the Non-Aligned Movement proves that they are the stooges of either superpower and are not genuine members of the Non-Aligned Movement.

Therefore at this critical juncture where the ongoing terrorism and invasions are threatening the lives of innocent people and the independence of undefended nations in every corner of the world, I request Your Excellency to use your good officers and influence to create unity. Solidarity of views and thoughts amongst the member countries of the Non-Aligned Movement, to be trusted as a natural non-aligned body, defending human rights against the so-called defender's human rights.

While I discuss human rights, it reminded me of the brutal invasion of the Soviet Union on December 27, 1979, and my dear beloved motherland; therefore, this opportunity was once being used to appeal to Your Excellency, H. E. Javier Perez-de-Cuellar, General Secretary of the UnitedNations and H. E. Peerzadah, General Secretary for Islamic conference, to do the needful to restore peace, independence, independence, freedom, national sovereignty and territorial sovereignty of my dear beloved motherland Afghanistan as soon as possible.

I avail of this opportunity to give Your Excellency the assurances of my highest consideration.

God bless you.

Yours truly,
Ahmed Afghan

cc:
HE Mr. Javier Perez de Cuellar, United Nations Secretary-General
HE Mr. Peerzadah, General Secretary of Islamic Conference

LETTER X

July 29, 1986

Mr. Mikhail Gorbachev
General Secretary
Communist Party of the Soviet Union
Kremlin, Moscow, USSR

Your Excellency,

I have the great honour to state that, all of a sudden, the invasion of the first 30,000 Soviet troops in Afghanistan during the three days of December 24–27, 1979, and Your Excellency's announcement in Vladivostok on July 28, 1986, about the withdrawal of about 8000/—out of 1,20,000/—Soviet troops in the remaining 152 days during the current year is the front page news item in the world Press.

The most important and palpable thing at this critical juncture is your decision and first commitment toward the complete withdrawal of the Soviet troops from Afghanistan.

Therefore, I earnestly hope that Your Excellency's announcement on the eve of the 7th round of Afghanistan-Pakistan proximity talks in Geneva under the auspices of the UN Secretary-General would also be supported by your colleague His Excellency Ronald Reagan, President of the United States of America, to achieve a fair, acceptable, and honourable political settlement of Afghanistan issue, and expedite the withdrawal of all the Soviet Union, to end a restoring peace, freedom, independence, national sovereignty, territorial sovereignty, and the nonaligned status of my dear, beloved motherland Afghanistan.

Therefore, once again, I avail of this opportunity to renew to Your Excellency the assurance of my highest consideration.

God bless you.

Yours truly,
Ahmed Afghan

cc:
HE Mr. Ronald Reagan, President of the United States of America, White House, Washington DC
HE Mr. Javier Perez Cuellar, General Secretary of United Nations, 866 United Nations Plaza, New York, USA

LETTER XI

August 20, 1986

HE Dr. Rupert Mugabe
Prime Minister of Zimbabwe
Office of Prime Minister Harare
Zimbabwe

Your Excellency,

I have the honour to wish you all the best and many successes in your heavy tasks and responsibilities ahead of you as Chairperson of the eight non-aligned summits.

By September 1, 1986, the leaders of 101 member countries will assemble in Harare, the capital of one of the most beautiful young African countries (Zimbabwe). And many significant political and economic issues of the world, such as Afghanistan, South Africa, the Middle East, the Iraq-Iran war, freezing of N. weapons, disarmament, the Star War, and peace in the world, will be on the agenda to be discussed at the summit.

Undoubtedly, the 25th anniversary of the movement in Harare will be a historic landmark if the leaders of the member countries prove that they are genuine members of the Non-Aligned Movement, not the stooges of either superpower.

Therefore, I express the hope that Your Excellency will succeed in building a strong and permanent bridge across the existing left and right wings of the movement and create unity and solidarity in view and thoughts among the member countries to move a solid and firm organization against all inequalities and injustice in the world organization against all inequalities and injustice in the world and acts as a real defender of human rights and peace in the world.

In regards to Afghanistan's critical issue, I may be permitted to express that, due to the differences and stubbornness of the two superpowers, all seven rounds of proximity talks between Afghanistan and Pakistan under the auspices of the UN Secretary-General have failed and thereby not yielded any positive results, The crisis, calamities and bloodshed are still going on in each & every nook of Afghanistan, and still, more than four million Afghans are living in an unbearable condition out their beloved motherland Afghanistan.

As for the withdrawal of the Soviet troops, H.E. Mr. Mekhail S. Gorbacheve, the Leader of the Soviet Union, on the eve of the eighth round of proximity talks between Afghanistan and Pakistan in Geneva, unilaterally announced the withdrawal of only 8000 troops up to the end of this year (152 days) from Afghanistan. That is also insignificant compared to more than 1,20,000 Soviet troops in Afghanistan.

There is no sign of any change in the stand and position of the Soviet Union regarding the withdrawal of all the Soviet troops from Afghanistan.

Therefore, under the critical circumstances, I take the courage to approach Your Excellency with a request to take some strong and positive steps, using your influence, and thereby convince the leaders of the member- countries that in a declaration urge the leaders of the superpowers (H. E. Mr. Ronald Reagan, President of the United States of America and H. E. Mr. Mikhail S. Gorbachev, General Secretary of the Communist Party of the Soviet Union) requesting for immediate join action to end the present crisis and bloodshed in Afghanistan and thus restore peace, freedom, independence, national sovereignty, national integration, territorial sovereignty, the nonaligned status of my dear beloved motherland Afghanistan.

I avail of this opportunity to give Your Excellency the assurances of my highest consideration.

God bless you.

Yours truly,
Ahmed Afghan

CC:
HE Mr. Javier Perez de Cuellar, United Nations Secretary-General
HE Mr. S. Peerzadah, General Secretary for Islamic Conference
HE Mr. Rajeev Gandhi, Prime Minister of India

My Warning litter About Terrorism and the Response from the International Air Transportation Association (IATA)

LETTER XII

Flat No. 92 9thFloor
Casablanca Apartment
Opp. World Trade Center
Cuffe Parade
Mumbai 400 005
India

September 8, 1986

HE Mr. Javier Pérez de Cuellar
United Nations Secretary-General
United Nations Organization
866 United Nations Plaza
New York, NY 10017
USA

Your Excellency,

Let me respectfully express that the Air Craft is the fastest and safest means of transportation in the world. Still, unfortunately in the last decade, by the inhuman terrorist actions of plane hijackers, the life of humanity has poorly been threatened with death.

On the contrary, we have been witnessing the loss of lives of more than a thousand innocent people in different bloody tragedies by hijacking planes in a distant corner of the world.

As a human being, I share my deepest and profound grief with all the bereaved families who have lost the precious lives of their dearest family members and those who were injured in the ill-fated Pan Am Flight 073 on September 5, 1986, in Karachi, I would therefore like to request Your Excellency to call in all the member countries in the Coming General Assembly of the United Nations, to start a worldwide struggle for eradicating all sorts of terrorist actions on the surface of the world, including the eradication of hijacking the planes.

To achieve this sacred goal successfully, I may also request Your Excellency to declare the year 1987 by adopting a resolution in the coming General Assembly of the United Nations as "World Wide Terrorism Eradication."

With the fulfillment of this objective, it would be for all the States and World Organization to take decisive and effective measures to reach this sacred and humane goal of eradicating the disastrous and bloody terrorism throughout the world successfully.

Indeed it is also a great pleasure to submit my personal information to the International Air Transportation Association (IATA) to tackle the deadly problem of hijacking planes worldwide.

A PROPOSAL FOR DEFUSING HIJACKING PLANS OF AIR CRAFTS

To end the perfidious and disastrous plans of the Air Crafts Hijackers without any Craft hijackers without any casualties and tensions to the crews and passengers on board, it is necessary to install an "Instant sleeping system" inside the plane, in a way that when the plane lands and comes to complete half, immediately the oxygen inside the aircraft should be cut off and instead, the instant sleeping gas should be released by a remote controller installed in the control tower.

To avoid damage to the plane after the completion of the first operation, it is necessary to build extra automatic escaping doors on different parts of the Air Crafts. These doors should also be only operated by remote control from the Control Tower.

I take this opportunity to assure Your Excellency of my highest consideration.

Sincerely yours,
Engineer Fazel Ahmed

CC:
HE Mr. Ronald Reagan, President of the United States of America
HE Mr. Mikhail S. Gorbachev, General Secretary of the Communist Party of the Soviet Union
HE Ms. Margaret Thatcher, Prime Minister of the United Kingdom
HE. Mr. The Leader, Communist Party of China (Mr. Hu Yao Beng)
HE International Air Transportation Association (IATA)
HE Mitterrand, President of the Government of France
HE Mr. Rajiv Gandhi, Prime Minister of India
HE Mr. Robert Mugabi, Prime Minister of Zimbabwe & Chairperson of the Non-Aligned Movement
HE Mr. S. S. Peerzada, General Secretary of Islamic Conference, Jeddah, Saudi Arabia

The letter from the International Air Transport Association in response to my letter, dated Sept 8th, 1986

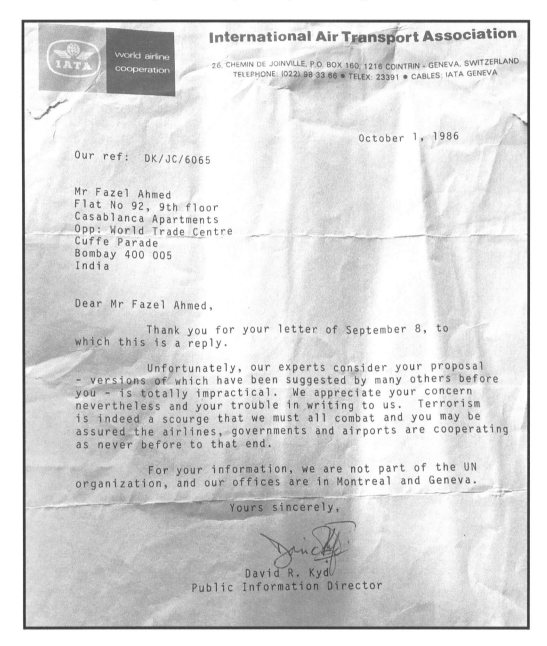

Yes, the International Air Transport Association (IATA) responded to my letter on October 1st, 1986. Still, unfortunately, my main concern wasn't addressed, which was requesting the General Assembly of the United Nations to pass a resolution to declare the year 1987 for the eradication of terrorism worldwide" what I meant by that was all the member countries of the United Nations should establish a Walch dog organization in their countries to keep an eye on activities of terrorists in their countries and annually submit the report of their findings to the United Nations General Assembly, given the reports a new guideline should have been adopted for the member countries how to stop the terrorist activities in the world.

Had that been adopted worldwide, it was possible that the sad tragedy of Sept 11, 2001, would not have happened.

LETTER XIII

October 14, 1986

HE Mr. Javier Pérez de Cuellar
United Nations Secretary-General
United Nations Organization
866 United Nations Plaza
New York, NY 10017
USA

Your Excellency,

May I have the pleasure and honour of extending my hearty congratulations on your re-election for the second five-year term as General Secretary of the United Nations?

Though in the last forty-one years of the United Nations, the speedy growth of population with different political and economic ideologies, accession of newly independent countries, the tremendous development of advanced Nuclear and other deadly sophisticated arms, the boom of high technology and the creation of new international organization such as NATO, OPIC, NAM, SAARO, Warsaw Pact and Islamic conference with different political and economic policies, have entirely changed the picture of the world and forced the United Nations to face difficulties and failures.

But it is a fact that despite the above-mentioned dramatic changes and madly struggle of the two superpowers for seeking world domination through an arms race on the earth and in outer space and their interferences in the United Nations, Your Excellency's endeavours, efforts, and stand in last five years as General Secretary of the United Nations to bring about peace and international economic order in all peace-loving people of the world.

The failure of the two superpowers to reach an accord in their summit meeting in Reykjavik on October 11–12, 1986, has once again proved that the leaders of the two superpowers are not genuinely willing to bring about peace and prosperity for the people of the world.

Therefore due to the differences and stubbornness of the leaders of the two superpowers and unquestionable right of the two superpowers and indisputable right of Veto, which the superpowers possess in the Secretary Council, and the enforcement of an ineffective forty-one years old Charter of the United Nations, in the unexpected advancement and the critical conditions Of the world at present, even Your Excellency's initiatives for peace and the resolutions adopted by the United Nations will be no effect.

At such a critical juncture, your re-election for the second term as General Secretary of the United Nations with many tasks and crucial problems, Sir, I give courage to myself. I humbly request you to make the United Nations an efficient and powerful world body. This is possible only by bringing together the leaders of the Soviet Union and the United States of America to reach a mutual understanding and an acceptable agreement to resolve their differences as soon as possible.

After achieving this, it would be possible to introduce some modifications to the United Nations Charter according to the desire and needs of the present and future world, thereby making the world a place for humanity to live in with peace, honour, dignity, and justice, equality, and prosperity.

In connection with my dear beloved motherland Afghanistan, I would like to express and reiterate that the withdrawal of only 8000 out of 1,20,000 Soviet troops from Afghanistan this month is insignificant; there is no sign of any change in the stand and position of the Soviet Union regarding the withdrawal of all their troops to give an end to the ongoing bloodshed in Afghanistan.

Therefore, I urge Your Excellency to take some strong and positive steps and immediate actions to convince the leader of the two superpowers to reach a rapid agreement regarding the positive, prestigious and acceptable political solution for the settlement of the Afghanistan issue.

I avail of this opportunity to assure Your Excellency of my highest consideration.

God bless you.

Yours Truly,
Ahmed Afghan

CC:
HE Dr. Rupert Mugabe, Prime Minister of Zimbabwe and Chairperson of the Nonaligned Movement
HE Mr. S. S. Peerzada, General Secretary for Islamic Conference

LETTER XIV

October 20, 1986

HE Mr. Rajiv Gandhi
Prime Minister of India
C/o Ministry of Foreign Affairs
New Delhi
India

Your Excellency,

I feel like approaching Your Excellency and stating respectfully that your firm and unshakable stand on South Africa, disarmament, terrorism, human right and many other such international issues have been "upright," as you rightly said in reply to a question of an Australian correspondent in Canberra on October 15, 1986, that "You are more tilted to the Soviet Union than the United States of America.

Many important matters relating to the present political and economic situation in the world will be discussed during the forthcoming visit of H. E. Mr. Mikhail Gorbachev, General Secretary of the Communist Party of the Soviet Union, to India on November 25, 1986. Thus the people of the world would be keenly watching and waiting to understand Your Excellency's stand on the Afghanistan issue.

Regarding the Afghanistan issue, I would like to draw your kind attention to the fact that the withdrawal of 8000 out of more than 1,20,000 Soviet Troops from Afghanistan this month is relatively insignificant in appearing to be merely a part of the Soviet Union's propaganda. However, there is no sign of any change in the stand of the Soviet Union regarding the withdrawal of all their troops from Afghanistan.

Hence the bloodshed, crisis and destruction are still going on in every corner of Afghanistan, and by day and night, at home or abroad, asleep or awake, the Afghans have no peace of mind.

I give once again the courage to myself and request, Your Excellency, that during the coming talks with the leader of the Soviet Union in New Delhi, please express your deep concern and unhappiness on the presence of the Soviet Troops and the ongoing bloodshed in Afghanistan and consequently stress for an immediate, prestigious and acceptable political settlement of Afghanistan issue.

I avail of this opportunity to thank you once again and wish you all the success in your tasks.

God bless you.

Yours truly,
Ahmed Afghan

CC:
HE Mr. Javier Perez de Cuellar United Nations Secretary-General United Nations Organization
HE Mr. S. S. Peerzada, General Secretary of the Islamic Conference
HE Dr. Robert Mugabe, Prime Minister of Zimbabwe & Chairperson of the Non-Aligned Movement

LETTER XV

Flat No. 92 Floor No. 9
Casablanca Apts.
Opp. World Trade Center
Cuffe Parade
Bombay-5
India

Dr. Najibullah
General Secretary
People's Party of Afghanistan
Center Committee

Respected Dr. Najibullah,

In continuation of my previous letters, as a son of my dear motherland, I have the honour to submit my view regarding the declaration of the 21st Plenum of the People's Democratic Party of Afghanistan held on December 30th, 1986.

It is an undeniable fact that the approach to creating a peaceful atmosphere on the dignified soil of Afghanistan is genuine and sincere national reconciliation. However, this sacred desire could only be fulfilled if the freedom, independence, national sovereignty, territorial sovereignty, national unity, and nonaligned status of dear Afghanistan were restored by the withdrawal of the Soviet troops and the national dignity and thereby the rights of the noble valorous nation of our beloved country be fully respected.

Thus, at this juncture that Your Excellency has invited the brave nation of Afghanistan for national reconciliation, it is my earnest desire to express very humbly that before any endeavours or efforts, a detailed programme for the withdrawal of the Soviet troops from the soil of Afghanistan and simultaneously the honourable return of all our refugee's brothers and sisters from Pakistan, Iran and other parts of the world, to their native-places must be worked out. Then, after procuring the consent of the concerned parties and thoroughly implementing the programme, the noble and courageous Afghan nation be invited for National reconciliation, and their valuable and destiny-making views to be sought for preparing a new constitution for a new regime in Afghanistan.

I also avail this opportunity to thank you and forward my first letter dated August 2nd, 1984, addressed to the general secretary of the United Nations, for your information as well as for the new constitution commission; I do hope it would be considered with other proposals of my dear countrymen/ women.

God bless you.

Yours truly,
Ahmed Afghan

CC:
HE Mr. Javier Perez de Cuellar United Nations Secretary-General United Nations Organization
HE Mr. S. S. Peerzada, General Secretary of the Islamic Conference
HE Dr. Robert Mugabe, Prime Minister of Zimbabwe & Chairperson of the Non-Aligned Movement
HE Mr. Ronald Reagan, President of the United States of America
HE Mr. Mikhail S. Gorbachev, General Secretary of the Communist Party of the Soviet Union
HE Ms. Margaret Thatcher, Prime Minister of the United Kingdom

Declaration of National Unity by PDPA in Dr. Najib's Era.

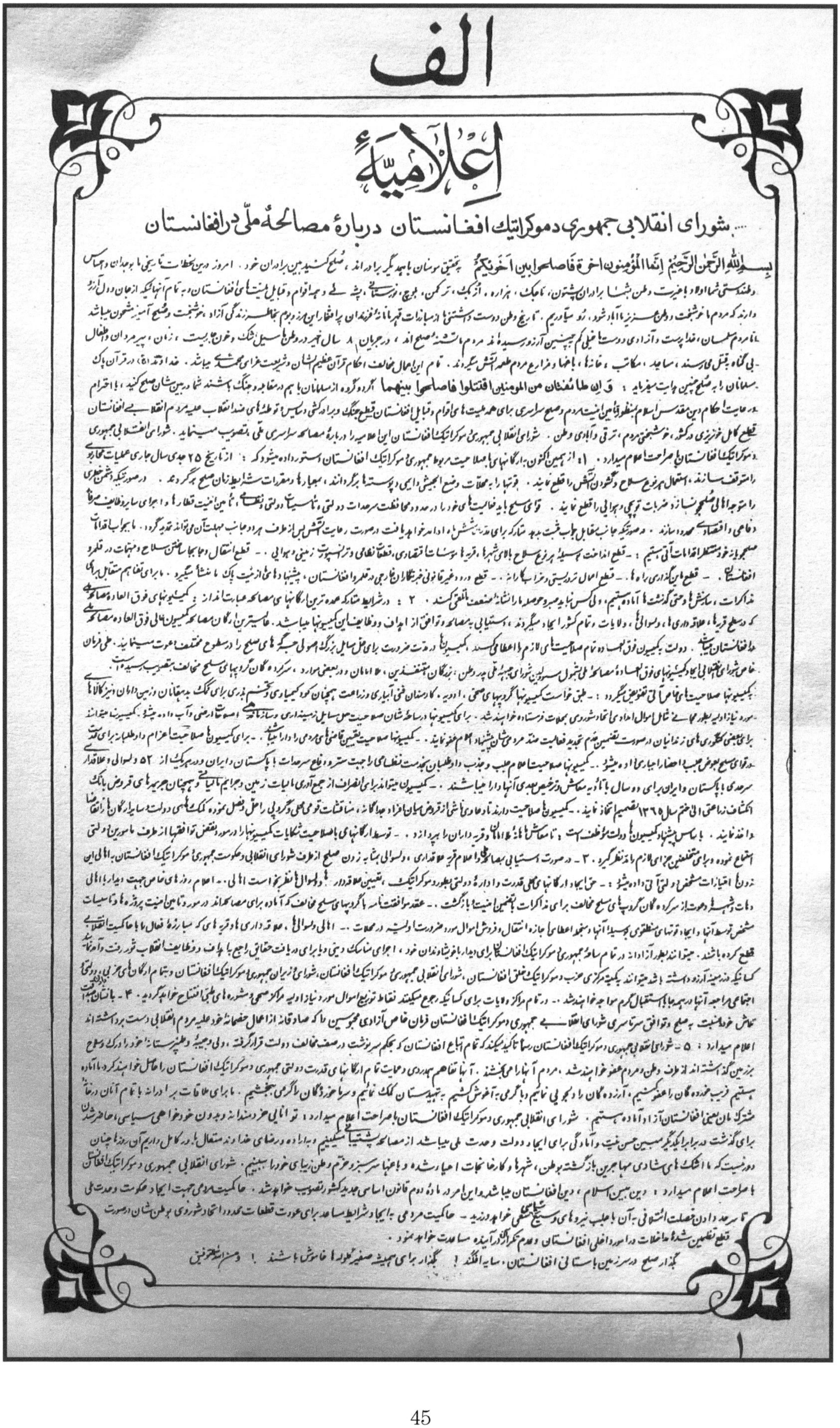
الف

اعلامیه

شورای انقلابی جمهوری دموکراتیک افغانستان دربارهٔ مصالحهٔ ملی در افغانستان

بسم الله الرحمن الرحیم انما المؤمنون اخوة فاصلحوا بین اخویکم بتحقیق مومنان با همدیگر برادر اند، صلح کنید بین برادران خود. امروز درین لحظات تاریخی با وجدان و احساس
وطندوستی شما اولاد باغیرت وطن، شما برادران پشتون، تاجک، هزاره، ازبک، ترکمن، بلوچ، نورستانی، پشه یی و همه اقوام و قبایل ملیت های افغانستان و به تمام آنهائیکه از جان و دل آرزو
دارند که مردم ما خوشبخت و وطن سرسبز و آباد شود، رو میآوریم. تاریخ وطن دوست داشتنی ما از مبارزات قهرمانانهٔ فرزندان پر افتخار این مرز و بوم بخاطر زندگی آزاد، خوشبخت و صلح آمیز مشحون میباشد
ما مردم مسلمان، خداپرست و آزادی دوست افغان کم چنین آرزو رسیده اند مردم ما تشنهٔ صلح اند، در جریان ۸ سال اخیر در وطن ما سیل اشک و خون جاریست، زنان، پیرمردان و اطفال
بی گناه بقتل میرسند، مساجد، مکاتب، خانه ها، باغها و مزارع مردم طعمهٔ آتش میگردند. تمام این اعمال مخالف احکام قرآن عظیم الشان و شریعت غرای محمدی میباشد. خداوند (ج) در قرآن پاک
مسلمانان را به صلح چنین هدایت میفرماید: وان طائفتان من المؤمنین اقتتلوا فاصلحوا بینهما اگر دو گروه از مسلمانان با هم در مقابله و جنگ باشند شما در بین شان صلح کنید. با احترام
و رعایت احکام دین مقدس اسلام بمنظور تأمین امنیت مردم و صلح سراسری برای همه ملیت ها، اقوام و قبایل افغانستان قطع جنگ و برادرکشی و مایوس ساختن توطئه های ضد انقلاب علیه مردم انقلابی افغانستان
قطع کامل خونریزی در کشور، خوشبختی مردم، ترقی و آبادی وطن. شورای انقلابی جمهوری دموکراتیک افغانستان این اعلامیه را دربارهٔ مصالحهٔ سراسری ملی بتصویب میرساند. شورای انقلابی جمهوری
دموکراتیک افغانستان با صراحت اعلام میدارد: ۱. از همین اکنون به ارگانهای با صلاحیت مربوط جمهوری دموکراتیک افغانستان دستور داده میشود که: از تاریخ ۲۵ جدی سال جاری عملیات محاربوی

LETTER XVI

March 21, 1987

Flat No. 92 Floor No. 9
Casablanca Apts.
Opp. World Trade Center
Cuffe Par
Bombay, India

HE Mr. Javier Perez de Cuellar
General Secretary
United Nations Organization
866 United Nations Plaza
New York, NY 10017
USA

Your Excellency,

It is indeed a great pleasure to say that at this happy stage, I have the news of substantial progress in the 8th round of proximity talks between Afghanistan and Pakistan on the Afghanistan issue from February 25 to March 10, 1987. It is an inspiring hope towards achieving a generally acceptable peace accord in the 9th round of proximity talks scheduled to be held in May or June 1987 in Geneva.

The present letter concludes a series of my sixteen peace-demanding letters and personal proposals for the political settlement of the Afghanistan issue.

Under my pen name, AHMED AFGHAN, I started with my first letter dated August 2, 1984, addressed to Your Excellency and the world leaders on different occasions as Council General of Democratic Republic of Afghanistan in Bombay from March 3, 1981, to November 1, 1985, as an Afghan residing in Bombay. Therefore, I avail myself of expressing my sincere and hearty gratitude to Your Excellency, H.E. Diego Cordovez, the United Nations, Non-Aligned Movement Conference, Islamic Conference, Peace-loving people and Organization of the World for their untiring and indefatigable humanitarian endeavour towards the hopeful fulfillment of a peace accord to restore the independence, freedom, national sovereignty, territorial sovereignty, national integration and the nonaligned status of my beloved country, and those of my Afghan brothers and sisters. They have continuously struggled and sacrificed their lives to prove that the Afghans have a proud history of taking what is theirs right through struggles in the last seven years.

There is no doubt that the coming Geneva accord will be another landmark in the annals of the United Nations and will be regarded and recorded in the history of Afghanistan and the world.

Therefore to achieve this sacred desire, I humbly appeal once again to Your Excellency, leaders of the two superpowers, world organizations, and all concerned parties, that the coming talks in Geneva should not be allowed to face frustration and failure. Instead, it must end to a generally acceptable peace accord for the settlement of the Afghanistan issue, as well as creating the special relief fund centers for the return and payment of Afghan refugees to their native places and extending unconditional economic as well as technical aid for rehabilitation, reconstruction, and above all, development of my dear beloved motherland Afghanistan.

It is a fact that the peace accord will be the beginning of a process leading to the end of the ongoing imposed crisis bloodshed in Afghanistan. However, achieving complete and successful peace in Afghanistan will depend only on the honesty, sincerity and vigilance of all the parties involved in implementing the peace accord.

Thus in this connection, I very humbly appeal to all the parties involved to maintain their vigilance and be sincere and honest in successfully implementing the coming peace accord. I also appeal to everyone to strongly express that the keys to immediate and perpetual peace and prosperity in Afghanistan lie in a firm and unshakable unity, solidarity and integrity among all my loving Afghan brothers and sisters against their common enemies. Otherwise, Afghanistan in the South Asian region will also have the same fate as Lebanon in the Middle East, facing endless bloodshed, brother killing, crisis and destruction.

I avail of this opportunity to assure Your Excellency of my highest consideration. A new early acknowledgment of this letter will be highly appreciated.

God bless you.

Yours truly,
Engineer Fazel Ahmed, MSc.
Ex-Consul General
The Democratic Republic of Afghanistan in Bombay

CC
HE Dr. Najibullah, General Secretary for the People's Democratic Party of Afghanistan
HE Mr. Mikhail Gorbachev, General Secretary of the Communist Party of the Soviet Union
HE Mr. Ronald Reagan, President of the United States of America
HE Mr. Deigo Gordoviz, Under Secretary to the United Nations
HE Mr. S. Sharifuddin Peerzadah, General Secretary to Islamic Conference
HE Mr. Rajiv Gandhi, Prime Minister of the Republic of India
HE General Zia-ul-Haq, President of the Republic of Pakistan
HE Mr. Deng Xiaoping, leader of the People's Republic of China
HE Mr. Rebert Mugabe, Prime Minister of Zimbabwe and Chairperson of the Non-Aligned Movement
HE Imam Ayatollah Khomeini, Revolutionary Leader of the Islamic Republic of Iran.

The continuation of my genuine non-stop struggles since 1987 in Canada for the cause of independence, freedom and peace in my beloved motherland Afghanistan.

LETTERS AND PROPOSALS SENT FROM CANADA

LETTER I

December 27, 1987

Engineer Fazel Ahmed, MSc
132 West 48th Avenue Vancouver,
BC, Canada V5Y 2Y7
Mr. Javier Perez de Cuellar
United Nations Secretary-General
United Nations Organization
866 United Nations Plaza
New York, NY 10017
USA

Your Excellency,

May I have the pleasure and honour to express that during the three-day Summit Talks between Mikhail Gorbachev and Ronald Reagan on December 10, 11, and 12, 1987, in Washington DC.

The signing of a treaty to eliminate the superpowers' medium-range nuclear missiles was a landmark in the history of the world. Still, it was also very disappointing and sad to learn that due to the differences of opinion of the leaders of the two superpowers, the talks made little progress toward yielding an acceptable and prestigious solution for the political settlement of the Afghanistan issue.

Indeed it would have been desirable to end the ongoing bloodshed and destruction in my dear country, Afghanistan. Therefore, on the sad occasion of the ninth anniversary of the invasion of Afghanistan (December 27, 1979), my dear fellow citizens mourn and, along with other peace-loving people of the world, condemn the open and brutal invasion of the Soviet Union into Afghanistan. Therefore, I once again, as a servant of my dear Afghan brothers and sisters, very humbly request Your Excellency to express your most profound concern and unhappiness on the failure of the talks between the two leaders on the Afghanistan issue.

Further, I would request that you urge the leaders of the USSR and the USA to reach a favourable mutual agreement to restore peace, independence, freedom, national sovereignty, territorial sovereignty, national integration and nonaligned status of Afghanistan as soon as possible.

I also humbly appeal to the Congress of the United States of America to ask the Soviet Union to submit a generally acceptable timetable for withdrawing their troops from Afghanistan before the treaty of medium-range nuclear missiles is ratified by the American Congress.

Although I had concluded my cries and appeals to the world leaders in my previous Letter No. XVI addressed to Your Excellency on March 21, 1987; on this occasion, it is my duty to appeal to the world leaders to join the cries of all peace-loving Afghans and strongly condemn the Soviet Union's invasion of the beloved motherland of all heroic and patriotic Afghans.

I seize this opportunity to assure Your Excellency of my highest consideration. An early acknowledgment of this letter would be greatly appreciated.

God bless you.

Yours truly,
Ahmed Afghan

CC:
Mr. Mikhail Gorbachev, General Secretary of the Communist Party of the Soviet Union
Mr. Ronald Reagan, President of the United States of America
Mr. Diego Cordovas, Undersecretary of United Nations
The Honorable Chairman of the Senate of the United States of America
The Honorable Chairman of the House of Representatives of the United States of America
Mr. Rajiv Gandhi, Prime Minister of India
Mr. S. Shahfuddin Pearzaduh, General Secretary to the Islamic Conference
Mr. Robert Mugabe, Prime Minister of Zimbabwe and Chairperson of the Non-Aligned Movement
HE Imam Ayatollah Khomeini, Revolutionary Leader of the Islamic Republic of Iran
HE General Zia-ul- Haq, President of the Republic of Pakistan
HE The Leader of the People's Republic of China
Honourable Brian Mulroney, Prime Minister of Canada

LETTER II

December 6, 2008

His Excellency Mr. Giulio Terzi,
Ambassador of Italy to the United Nations UN Headquarters
First Avenue at 46ᵗʰ Street
New York, NY 10017

Your Excellency,

The Attached Proposal for a fundamental change in Afghanistan's government is one of my articles written to be used as a tool for vital and honourable individuals such as yourself and strong organizations such as the United Nations to consider. Therefore, I hope you and your good office find it informative and helpful while making significant decisions regarding Afghanistan shortly.

I apologize for not translating the article into English. I humbly request your highly qualified translators to solve this significant article in English and bring the same to Your Excellency's attention.

I am available to thank you and express good wishes on your essential tasks in Afghanistan.

I am looking forward to hearing from you. I wish you and your kind office a happy holiday season.

God bless you.

Yours sincerely,
Engineer Fazel Ahmed Afghan

Cc:
His Excellency Mr. Barack Obama, President-Elect of the United States of America
His Excellency Mr. Hamed Karzai, President of Afghanistan—c/o
Honourable Mr. Zaher Tanin, Afghanistan's Ambassador to the United Nations
Honorable Kai Eide, Special Representative of the UN Secretary-General for Afghanistan

A Proposal for Fundamental Changes in the Government of Afghanistan by Engineer Fazel Ahmed Afghan

As is known to everybody, the slogan of President Obama during the campaign was "Change." Of course, the purpose of the motto of change was not merely the changing of a white President to a black President. Still, his sincere desire was to introduce fundamental changes in the scattered socioeconomic, political and military status of America at the national and international levels so that he could introduce rapid change.

As a result, all-sided developments not only regain the prestige of the United States of America throughout the world but also elevate it. In other words, the slogan of change which reflects Mr. Barack Obama's sacred national goals has made him a beloved leader to both white and black Americans and enabled him to become the leader of the most powerful nation on Earth and to govern this nation.

Indeed, the American nation, by electing Mr. Obama, proved to the world that their national interests are higher than colour, minority and majority. That purity, sincerity, honesty, knowledge, patriotism and broadmindedness are qualities which constitute the character of Mr. Obama and which gained him success in the election at both national and international levels. In addition, he stood free of the old and unpopular contradictions and forgotten inhuman values.

Unfortunately, the oppressed nation of Afghan would soon face once again, consciously or unconsciously, a vital national trial, that is to say, that contrary to what we observed in the American election, many unworthy personas are planning to hold an election, using the slogans of ethnic, religion and region or cheating people by misinterpreting the articles of the constitution.

They aim to collect votes from illiterate, uninformed and ignorant people to establish themselves as winners. This is happening at a time when the national infrastructure is destroyed; the nation is fighting an imposed war, the census has not been taken, local consultative assemblies have not been established, security does not exist, millions of refugees are still abroad, corruption, bribery, and injustice prevail, Afghan culture is under foreign domination, and there is no law and order.

There is no unity between the house and the senate, and the election commission has significant differences between the President of the Republic and the home. Irresponsible attacks of foreign forces continue on the defenceless villages and towns, and suicidal attacks kill many innocent people. Mr. Karzai is fighting with the united front and heroin production, and its illegal trade continues as before.

This unworthy governing group cares only for its interests, stamping the national interests; they do not believe in social equality, human dignity, human rights, purity, sincerity, honesty and patriotism. Instead, they struggle merely for power and money, cheating uninformed and ignorant people.

In recognition of the above problems and the fact that the destiny of the oppressed Afghan nation has been determined from abroad during the past thirty years. The national social code by which the country resolved its national problems by convening the traditional great national assembly (Loya Jirga) is no longer feasible.

The nation at this time cannot determine its destiny, nor can the foreign powers impose their will on the Afghan country. It is therefore essential that the Afghan nation, especially the Afghan intellectual group, those with purity, honesty, patriotism and experience, who have not stampeded human rights and enjoy the trust of the United Nations, should take the initiative to implement the "Proposal for the Fundamental Changes in the Government of Afghanistan."

Taking into consideration the internal and regional conditions included in the proposal, it is emphasized that the views and findings of the United Nations mission consisting of 15 members, including the big powers, such as the USA, Russian Federation and the People's Republic of China, which has recently visited Afghanistan, should also be considered. It is expected that the mission has touched on the realities and the numerous problems Afghanistan has been facing during the past thirty years, as well as the foreign interferences in Afghanistan.

Before making a quick conclusion and decision, the mission should read the "Proposal for Fundamental Changes in the Government of Afghanistan," which suggests the convening of a national inter-Afghan conference and the Afghan representative national (Loya Jirga). Then after the approval of the security council submits its recommendations to the Karzi government and the coordinating committee of the inter-Afghan conference.

Mr. Hamed Karzai, the President of the Islamic Republic of Afghanistan, too, considers his conscious, moral, religious, Islamic and international obligations to protect his honour and the salvation of the motherland.

A country which he has inherited from his ancestors and which cannot tolerate misery and maltreatment anymore. He should accept that the forthcoming election based on the constitution is improper, unjust and in contradiction with the social justice, national interest of the country and the world's opinion.

It is therefore respectfully suggested that a different way should be sought, which is the "Proposal for Fundamental Changes in the Government of Afghanistan," by which the oppressed Afghan nation, as well as the entire world, would enjoy peace and comfort during the forthcoming years. In other words, based on article (64), item (8), chapter III of the constitution concerning (the Presidency) and chapter IX on (emergency), the President, after the approval of the national assembly, should declare a crisis in the country due to the reason of dominant insecurity, terrorism and suicidal attacks in many parts of the country.

He should demand from the United Nations the convening of the Inter-Afghan National Conference, as well as the Great National Representative Assembly (Loya Jirga).

A-Calling for inter-Afghan Conference.

1. Under the current challenging conditions, the traditional (Loya Jirga) cannot be convened; therefore, it is necessary to demand the moral and financial cooperation of the United Nations to invite and convene an Inter-Afghan Conference consisting of 400 Afghan patriotic scholars and intellectuals whose names have not been listed as violators of human rights. They would relatively represent the Afghan societies in and out of Afghanistan as a substitute for the traditional Loya Jirga (Representative Loya Jirga).

This group of 400 should then elect a group of highly educated and respected 100 Afghans by free, direct and secret voting from among themselves, supervised by a non-Afghan institution, trustworthy and acceptable to Afghans. The non-Afghan institution would manage and execute the election using a computer-based method. Finally, the elected group of 100 would form and convene the "Inter-Afghan Conference."

2. The United Nations selected 20 neutral and nonaligned Afghan scholars by direct and secret computerized voting, performed by a non-Afghan institution trusted and approved by Afghans, to participate. Of the proposed 400 members, "Representative Loya Jirga." Then six persons from these 20 persons will be selected by a similar computerized system to participate in the 100-member "Inter-Afghan Conference," held in Kabul, the capital of Afghanistan.

The selected six persons will be then introduced to the special envoy of the United Nations as members of the "coordinating committee" of the 100 members "Inter-Afghan National Conference" so that under the United Nations auspices and financial aid, members of the proposed "Representatives Loya Jirga," consisting of scholars and intellectuals are selected to begin their task force.

Members of the "coordinating committee" have equal rights and privileges of voting and candidacy like other members of the proposed "Inter-Afghan Conference" and "Representative Loya Jirga." Therefore, the number of the members of the proposed "Representative Loya Jirga," including the members of the "coordinating committee" and "Inter-Afghan Conference," are introduced to be included as follows.

3. All the members of the Bonn Conference, representing the Rome Conference, Peshawar Conference, Cypress Conference and the Northern United Front.

4. The President of the National Assembly, his two assistants and the two secretaries of the National Assembly, and 25 members of the National assembly.

5. The President of the Senate, his two assistants and the two secretaries, together with ten members of ahhe Senate.

6. Presidents of the Provincial Assemblies.

7. Ten people are representing the Taliban movement.

8. Ten people representing the Islamic Party of Hekmatyar.

9. Ten people represent the People's Democratic Party, with five from the "Khalq faction" and five from the "Parcham faction."

10. Ten people represent the "Jalaluddin Haqqani Party."

11. Twenty people represent the current Government Executive and Judiciary sections.

12. Sixty persons represent various Universities in Afghanistan. The Ministry of Higher Education will determine the number of each University concerning the number of Academic boards each.

13. Eighty persons representing various nonaligned and nonpartisan Inter-Afghan conferences held in America and Europe during the past seven years (the number of shares of each meeting will be determined concerning the number of participants in each panel).

14. Finally, about seventy people representing the Afghan Technocrats were included in the United Nations lists of 1993 and 1994.

B: Duties of the Proposed "Representative Loya Jirga"

1. 1. Selecting the members of the "Inter-Afghan Conference."

2. 2. Ratifying the resolutions of the "National Inter-Afghan Conference."

3. 3. With the exclusion of seventy-six persons (detailed in the duties of the "National Inter-Afghan Conference"), extending the existence and authorities of the current National Assembly and the Senate of Afghanistan for five years.

C: Duties and Functions of the Proposed "National Inter-Afghan Conference."

**The National Inter-Afghan Conference will be held in Kabul under a temporary Chairmanship of the special envoy of the United Nations, observing a special Islamic ceremony and will perform the following duties after the approval of the plan and procedure of the Conference.

1. Electing the President and two secretaries of the Inter-Afghan Conference by free and secret voting among three candidates.

2. Approving the Agenda and procedure of the Conference.

3. Discuss and make decisions on the following proposals.

- To eliminate the regional crisis, Afghanistan should be recognized as a buffer state between the neighbouring countries so that neither Afghanistan attacks another country nor another country attacks Afghanistan, and Afghanistan should not be used as a means to attack another country.

- Afghanistan should be recognized as a free, independent and non-aligned country, active and not indifferent.

- Under the prevailing conditions, due to the lacking of sufficient military and police forces, Afghanistan cannot fight terrorists and foreign suicidal attackers. therefore it would be necessary to reform the Afghan National Army and Police based on the former (1978) tradition of two years of "National Obligatory Service."

- Security and stability are essential for implementing socio-economic-political programs; therefore, severe measures should be adopted to collect arms from armed civilians (NGOs) and warlords.

  The Government should declare and warn that all forms of arms, excluding small pistols and hunting guns, must be returned to the Government free of cost or in exchange for food, clothing, agricultural seeds, fertilizers or industrial tools; otherwise, the Government would use force to collect the arms from the public and those not cooperating would be punished.

  In Kabul, as well as other cities, arms should be collected from all civilians, warlords, Afghan and non-Afghan institutions and NGOs. Furthermore, the security of the towns, Government organizations, private institutions, foreign embassies, Consulates and commercial agencies should be guaranteed by the joint UN and Afghan forces based on bilateral agreements.

  Parties not accepting the Government order should be seriously punished.

- Appointing an authorized commission among experienced Afghan experts to draft five-five years of developmental plans for 25 years with the cooperation of foreign Experts.

- Considering the socio-economic-military and human resources conditions of the country and the priorities. This plan should be prepared within six to nine months to be submitted to foreign investors and international institutions to attract foreign financial and technical aid to reconstruct Afghanistan's infrastructure.

- Appointing twenty scholars consisting of economic, military, social and political experts by free and secret voting from the "Inter-Afghan National Conference" members to be stationed at the United Nations in New York for five years. They will function as a bridge and liaison between the United Nations and the Government of Afghanistan for coordinating various functions.

- Gradual coordination of the implementation of the process of democracy and the free market with the process of socio-economic development and law enforcement in all Government and private sectors; searching for ways and means to attract and encourage the participation of Afghan societies in Government affairs, projects and the process of reconstruction in particular.

- Accepting the theory of creating government cooperatives to compete with the internal and external private sectors in matters such as the supply of food (i.e. tea, sugar, edible oil, benzine, gas, flour, and wheat) and reorganizing the old system of distributing "Coupons" to the Government employees, teachers, contract employees and military officers.

- Creating a reasonable policy for avoiding the cultivation, processing and illegal sale and trade of opium; creating work and employment for the peasants engaged in such matters; tracing and punishing internal and foreign heroin dealers; implementing heavy punishments like those in Saudi Arabia on the dealers; encouraging landowners to cultivate such substitute as saffron, cotton, sugar cane, beetroot, horticulture, raising livestock, poultry, ice-making factories in the main cities and simple ones in the villages; using solar energy and small generators for creating energy; giving long-term loans for the realization of those projects: establishing agricultural Cooperatives and small factories for processing food items, fruits, candies and the like.

- Researching the claims of Afghanistan and the Russian Federation in connection to the former demand for the war compensation/reparation and the latter demand for the payment of the loans given to former puppet Governments and reaching a final solution under the auspices of the security council.

- Finding a solution to the problem of "Pashtunistan," Pashtuns are our brothers sharing the same religion, language, culture and traditions; this land was separated from Afghanistan, and an imposed line was drawn to separate the two brothers.

- However, we want a choice of self-determination for the Pashtuns and Balouches, preserving the territorial integrity of Afghanistan. Therefore, we want to resolve the problem of the Durand Line by peaceful negotiation with Pakistan with the participation of the representatives of Pashtuns and Balouches under the auspices of the United Nations.

- A solid and final determination concerning amnesty or trial of the Afghan war criminals, violators of human rights and national traitors during the past thirty years.

- Searching for practical ways and means for the return of Afghan refugees from Pakistan and Iran and their settlement in uncultivated lands owned by the Government; giving each family a piece of land to build a house; building markets, health clinics, schools, police and security, digging deep wells, installing small diesel generators, building small factories and industries, etc. Under the supervision of the concerned ministry with the help of the world refugee and food organizations and initiating the work program for food.

- Providing settlement for Afghan Nomads (Kouchees) in various parts of the country, considering social justice and their living conditions; selling public lands under favourable terms at affordable prices and long-term payments and also issuing identification documents to the Nomads as a token to quit Nomadism.

- They are finding ways and means to financially support charity institutions such as (Small Islamic Bank) established in California, USA, (War-Torn Children and Ashiana) and the like for creating small industries like handmade items, arts and crafts and other low-priced items.

  Such projects would benefit poverty, unemployment, orphans, widows and maimed persons to make them self-efficient and attract national and international aid.

- Drafting a socio-economic-political and military guideline valid for five years for the future Government of Afghanistan.

- Making a firm decision concerning candidate Afghans who have double Nationality and legalized dual Nationality for all Afghan refugees living in Europe, America, Australia and Elsewhere.

- Revision of the Constitution, if necessary.

- Provisions for the election of the President of the Republic and his two assistants, twenty cabinet members, considering their educational background, practical experience, courage in decision making, righteousness and honesty.

  Selecting Provincial Governors from the 100 members of the "National Inter-Afghan Conference" by direct and secret voting from the three candidates for each position and giving preference to those Government candidates who are citizens of their respective provinces.

  For example, among the three candidates for the Governor of Herat, priority should be given to those who have better education, piety, courage, education, and experience and who are committed to implementing the policies of the central government.

- Finally, all the decisions concerning the election and the articles mentioned above about the functions and duties of the "National Inter-Afghan Conference" would be submitted to "Representative Loya Jirga" for ratification. Members of the "National

Inter-Afghan Conference" and the "coordinating committee" will also participate in the "Representative Loya Jirga."

- The First of Jouza 1388 (May 21, 2009) is the termination date of the Presidency of Mr. Karzai. On the completion of the two months emergency, "Representative Loya Jirga" would convene to ratify the decisions of the "National Inter-Afghan Conference." Thus a new chapter would open in the history of Afghanistan.

- After the ratification of the decisions of the "National Inter-Afghan Conference" by "Representative Loya Jirga," the present National Assembly and Senate would be dissolved, except for the members of the cabinet (20) and provincial Governors and twenty Afghan experts for the United Nations.

- Members of the "Representative Loya Jirga" would replace those dissolved for five years; the new President would choose his "Selective Representatives" from the members of the "Inter-Afghan Conference" under article (84), item (3) of the constitution; provincial assemblies each would elect a new chairman.

- At the "Representative Loya Jirga," after the completion of the procedures for ratifying and dissolving during the two months of Hamal and Saour (March 21–May 21), the last day of Mr. Karzai's Presidency is Saour 30th (April 21), under article (61), chapter III of the constitution; on the first day of Djouza 1388 (May 22, 2009) Mr. Karzai will transfer the powers to the new leadership and administration in an official ceremony.

- Mention must be made that from among living abroad, those who are selected to go to Afghanistan as members of the "Representative Loya Jirga" they should serve with righteousness, honesty, responsibility, concern for human rights, love and devotion for Motherland, caring for national interests and not for personal interests.

In addition, they should persuade and encourage other Afghans living abroad to return and serve their country with whatever means available. It is hoped that the Afghan Government or International Institutions will provide for the livelihood of those returning to perform in Afghanistan.

We seek help from Almighty God for success.

LETTER III

August 30, 2009

His Excellency Mr. Jean–Maurice Ripert
Ambassador Extraordinary and
Plenipotentiary Permanent Representative
of France to the United Nations

Your Excellency,

Indeed it is a great pleasure for my Afghan citizens and me to hear that your government will soon be hosting an international conference in Paris to discuss the outcome of the recent presidential election in Afghanistan, the future of Afghanistan and the international organizations working in the country.

There has been a great discussion, and a spotlight has been placed by the global community and the people of Afghanistan on issues such as widespread corruption in the current electoral process, along with views that both front runners in the presidential election have been associated with corruption, and that their government will be backed by or may include deemed warlords and alleged human right violations.

Accordingly, under such conditions and ill support of the first round of elections, it is clear that there is no hope and guarantees that either one of such candidates or the second round of the presidential election will be fruitful in bringing to power someone that will have the democratic support of the people of Afghanistan and be able to encourage peace and stability and move the country towards prosperity.

On the contrary, it means that in the coming five years, through the term of an unsupported government based on fundamentally corrupt elections, billions of dollars of foreign assistance and aid will once again be wasted at the hands of corruption, and thousands of innocent Afghans and foreign troops will be killed through continued violence in instability. In addition, the drug lords will continue to gain power and generate wealth for themselves and their warlord associates through the harvest of illegal drugs, which will fall into the hands of innocent Afghans and lead to the continued rise of social issues such as drug addiction.

To prevent such a colossal defeat for a country on the brink of survival and hope and one that, after decades of misfortune, has The chance for success, we, as members of a collaborative global community, must take action now.

Therefore, as a member of this global community and as an Afghan deeply in support of the success of my country's future and initiatives such as those proposed in Paris, I believe the best solution to bring peace and stability in Afghanistan and the region as well as establishing a responsible government in Afghanistan is to evaluate alternative proposals and reach a new and prosperous path that will be supported by the democratic people of Afghanistan as well as the global community.

One such suggestion is that of mine, dated December 20, 2008, under "A PROPOSAL FOR FUNDAMENTAL CHANGES IN THE GOVERNMENT OF AFGHANISTAN."

This proposal has already been shared with your kind office and other respected and honourable members of the United Nations Security Council.

Here once again I avail this opportunity to draw to you and your colleagues' kind attention and the member country representatives that will participate in the upcoming conference in Paris to my said proposal.

I do hope and trust that you will find some points of benefit and usefulness to be considered as you progress through upcoming discussions on the current electoral and political issues facing Afghanistan. When faced with such circumstances of importance, we must pursue and explore every opportunity provided to us that may assist in finding a solution of mutual benefit to all the interested parties and especially the people of Afghanistan.

I avail this opportunity to thank you and express good wishes on your crucial tasks in Afghanistan.

I humbly attach the proposal for your reading and consideration.

Thank you for your kind attention, and God bless you.

Yours sincerely,
Mr. Engineer Fazel Ahmed Afghan

A PROPOSAL FOR FUNDAMENTAL CHANGES IN THE GOVERNMENT OF AFGHANISTAN BY ENGINEER FAZEL AHMED AFGHAN

As is known to everybody, the slogan of President Obama during the campaign was "Change." Of course, the purpose of the motto of change was not merely the changing of a white President to a black President. Still, his sincere desire was to introduce fundamental changes in the scattered socioeconomic, political and military status of America at the national and international levels so that he could introduce rapid change.

As a result, all-sided developments not only regain the prestige of the United States of America throughout the world but also elevate it. In other words, the slogan of change which reflects Mr. Barack Obama's sacred national goals has made him a beloved leader to both white and black Americans and enabled him to become the leader of the most powerful nation on Earth and to govern this nation.

Indeed, the American nation, by electing Mr. Obama, proved to the world that their national interests are higher than colour, minority and majority. That purity, sincerity, honesty, knowledge, patriotism and broadmindedness are qualities which constitute the character of Mr. Obama and which gained him success in the election at both national and international levels. In addition, he stood free of the old and unpopular contradictions and forgotten inhuman values.

Unfortunately, the oppressed nation of Afghan would soon face once again, consciously or unconsciously, a vital national trial, that is to say, that contrary to what we observed in the American election, many unworthy personas are planning to hold an election, using the slogans of ethnic, religion and region or cheating people by misinterpreting the articles of the constitution.

They aim to collect votes from illiterate, uninformed and ignorant people to establish themselves as winners. This is happening at a time when the national infrastructure is destroyed; the nation is fighting an imposed war, the census has not been taken, local consultative assemblies have not been established, security does not exist, millions of refugees are still abroad, corruption, bribery, and injustice prevail, Afghan culture is under foreign domination, and there is no law and order.

There is no unity between the house and the senate, and the election commission has significant differences between the President of the Republic and the home. Irresponsible attacks of foreign forces continue on the defenceless villages and towns, and suicidal attacks kill many innocent people. Mr. Karzai is fighting with the united front and heroin production, and its illegal trade continues as before.

This unworthy governing group cares only for its interests, stamping the national interests; they do not believe in social equality, human dignity, human rights, purity, sincerity, honesty and patriotism. Instead, they struggle merely for power and money, cheating uninformed and ignorant people.

In recognition of the above problems and the fact that the destiny of the oppressed Afghan nation has been determined from abroad during the past thirty years. The national social code by which the country resolved its national problems by convening the traditional great national assembly (Loya Jirga) is no longer feasible.

The nation at this time cannot determine its destiny, nor can the foreign powers impose their will on the Afghan country. It is therefore essential that the Afghan nation, especially the Afghan intellectual group, those with purity, honesty, patriotism and experience, who have not stampeded human rights and enjoy the trust of the United Nations, should take the initiative to implement the "Proposal for the Fundamental Changes in the Government of Afghanistan."

Taking into consideration the internal and regional conditions included in the proposal, it is emphasized that the views and findings of the United Nations mission consisting of 15 members, including the big powers, such as the USA, Russian Federation and the People's Republic of China, which has recently visited Afghanistan, should also be considered. It is expected that the mission has touched on the realities and the numerous problems Afghanistan has been facing during the past thirty years, as well as the foreign interferences in Afghanistan.

Before making a quick conclusion and decision, the mission should read the "Proposal for Fundamental Changes in the Government of Afghanistan," which suggests the convening of a national inter-Afghan conference and the Afghan representative national (Loya Jirga). Then after the approval of the security council submits its recommendations to the Karzi government and the coordinating committee of the inter-Afghan conference.

Mr. Hamed Karzai, the President of the Islamic Republic of Afghanistan, too, considers his conscious, moral, religious, Islamic and international obligations to protect his honour and the salvation of the motherland.

A country which he has inherited from his ancestors and which cannot tolerate misery and maltreatment anymore. He should accept that the forthcoming election based on the constitution is improper, unjust and in contradiction with the social justice, national interest of the country and the world's opinion.

It is therefore respectfully suggested that a different way should be sought, which is the "Proposal for Fundamental Changes in the Government of Afghanistan," by which the oppressed Afghan nation, as well as the entire world, would enjoy peace and comfort during the forthcoming years. In other words, based on article (64), item (8), chapter III of the constitution concerning (the Presidency) and chapter IX on (emergency), the President, after the approval of the national assembly, should declare a crisis in the country due to the reason of dominant insecurity, terrorism and suicidal attacks in many parts of the country.

He should demand from the United Nations the convening of the Inter-Afghan National Conference, as well as the Great National Representative Assembly (Loya Jirga).

A-Calling for inter-Afghan Conference.

1. Under the current challenging conditions, the traditional (Loya Jirga) cannot be convened; therefore, it is necessary to demand the moral and financial cooperation of the United Nations to invite and convene an Inter-Afghan Conference consisting of 400 Afghan patriotic scholars and intellectuals whose names have not been listed as violators of human rights. They would relatively represent the Afghan societies in and out of Afghanistan as a substitute for the traditional Loya Jirga (Representative Loya Jirga).

This group of 400 should then elect a group of highly educated and respected 100 Afghans by free, direct and secret voting from among themselves, supervised by a non-Afghan institution, trustworthy and acceptable to Afghans. The non-Afghan institution would manage and execute the election using a computer-based method. Finally, the elected group of 100 would form and convene the "Inter-Afghan Conference."

2. The United Nations selected 20 neutral and nonaligned Afghan scholars by direct and secret computerized voting, performed by a non-Afghan institution trusted and approved by Afghans, to participate. Of the proposed 400 members, "Representative Loya Jirga." Then six persons from these 20 persons will be selected by a similar computerized system to participate in the 100-member "Inter-Afghan Conference," held in Kabul, the capital of Afghanistan.

The selected six persons will be then introduced to the special envoy of the United Nations as members of the "coordinating committee" of the 100 members "Inter-Afghan National Conference" so that under the United Nations auspices and financial aid, members of the proposed "Representatives Loya Jirga," consisting of scholars and intellectuals are selected to begin their task force.

Members of the "coordinating committee" have equal rights and privileges of voting and candidacy like other members of the proposed "Inter-Afghan Conference" and "Representative Loya Jirga." Therefore, the number of the members of the proposed "Representative Loya Jirga," including the members of the "coordinating committee" and "Inter-Afghan Conference," are introduced to be included as follows.

3. All the members of the Bonn Conference, representing the Rome Conference, Peshawar Conference, Cypress Conference and the Northern United Front.

4. The President of the National Assembly, his two assistants and the two secretaries of the National Assembly, and 25 members of the National assembly.

5. The President of the Senate, his two assistants and the two secretaries, together with ten members of the Senate.

6. Presidents of the Provincial Assemblies.

7. Ten people are representing the Taliban movement.

8. Ten people representing the Islamic Party of Hekmatyar.

9. Ten people represent the People's Democratic Party, with five from the "Khalq faction" and five from the "Parcham faction."

10. Ten people represent the "Jalaluddin Haqqani Party."

11. Twenty people represent the current Government Executive and Judiciary sections.

12. Sixty persons represent various Universities in Afghanistan. The Ministry of Higher Education will determine the number of each University concerning the number of Academic boards each.

13. Eighty persons representing various nonaligned and nonpartisan Inter-Afghan conferences held in America and Europe during the past seven years (the number of shares of each meeting will be determined concerning the number of participants in each panel).

14. Finally, about seventy people representing the Afghan Technocrats were included in the United Nations lists of 1993 and 1994.

B: Duties of the Proposed "Representative Loya Jirga"

1. Selecting the members of the "Inter-Afghan Conference."

2. Ratifying the resolutions of the "National Inter-Afghan Conference."

3. With the exclusion of seventy-six persons (detailed in the duties of the "National Inter-Afghan Conference"), extending the existence and authorities of the current National Assembly and the Senate of Afghanistan for five years.

C: Duties and Functions of the Proposed "National Inter-Afghan Conference."

**The National Inter-Afghan Conference will be held in Kabul under
a temporary Chairmanship of the special envoy of the United Nations,
observing a special Islamic ceremony and will perform the following duties
after the approval of the plan and procedure of the Conference.

1. Electing the President and two secretaries of the Inter-Afghan Conference by free and secret voting among three candidates.

2. Approving the Agenda and procedure of the Conference.

3. Discuss and make decisions on the following proposals.

- To eliminate the regional crisis, Afghanistan should be recognized as a buffer state between the neighbouring countries so that neither Afghanistan attacks another country nor another country attacks Afghanistan, and Afghanistan should not be used as a means to attack another country.

- Afghanistan should be recognized as a free, independent and non-aligned country, active and not indifferent.

- Under the prevailing conditions, due to the lacking of sufficient military and police forces, Afghanistan cannot fight terrorists and foreign suicidal attackers. therefore it would be necessary to reform the Afghan National Army and Police based on the former (1978) tradition of two years of "National Obligatory Service."

- Security and stability are essential for implementing socio-economic-political programs; therefore, severe measures should be adopted to collect arms from armed civilians (NGOs) and warlords.

  The Government should declare and warn that all forms of arms, excluding small pistols and hunting guns, must be returned to the Government free of cost or in exchange for food, clothing, agricultural seeds, fertilizers or industrial tools; otherwise, the Government would use force to collect the arms from the public and those not cooperating would be punished.

  In Kabul, as well as other cities, arms should be collected from all civilians, warlords, Afghan and non-Afghan institutions and NGOs. Furthermore, the security of the towns,

Government organizations, private institutions, foreign embassies, Consulates and commercial agencies should be guaranteed by the joint UN and Afghan forces based on bilateral agreements.

Parties not accepting the Government order should be seriously punished.

- Appointing an authorized commission among experienced Afghan experts to draft five-five years of developmental plans for 25 years with the cooperation of foreign Experts.

- Considering the socio-economic-military and human resources conditions of the country and the priorities. This plan should be prepared within six to nine months to be submitted to foreign investors and international institutions to attract foreign financial and technical aid to reconstruct Afghanistan's infrastructure.

- Appointing twenty scholars consisting of economic, military, social and political experts by free and secret voting from the "Inter-Afghan National Conference" members to be stationed at the United Nations in New York for five years. They will function as a bridge and liaison between the United Nations and the Government of Afghanistan for coordinating various functions.

- Gradual coordination of the implementation of the process of democracy and the free market with the process of socio-economic development and law enforcement in all Government and private sectors; searching for ways and means to attract and encourage the participation of Afghan societies in Government affairs, projects and the process of reconstruction in particular.

- Accepting the theory of creating government cooperatives to compete with the internal and external private sectors in matters such as the supply of food (i.e. tea, sugar, edible oil, benzine, gas, flour, and wheat) and reorganizing the old system of distributing "Coupons" to the Government employees, teachers, contract employees and military officers.

- Creating a reasonable policy for avoiding the cultivation, processing and illegal sale and trade of opium; creating work and employment for the peasants engaged in such matters; tracing and punishing internal and foreign heroin dealers; implementing heavy punishments like those in Saudi Arabia on the dealers; encouraging landowners to cultivate such substitute as saffron, cotton, sugar cane, beetroot, horticulture, raising livestock, poultry, ice-making factories in the main cities and simple ones in the villages; using solar energy and small generators for creating energy; giving long-term loans for the realization of those projects: establishing agricultural Cooperatives and small factories for processing food items, fruits, candies and the like.

- Researching the claims of Afghanistan and the Russian Federation in connection to the former demand for the war compensation/reparation and the latter demand for the payment of the loans given to former puppet Governments and reaching a final solution under the auspices of the security council.

- Finding a solution to the problem of "Pashtunistan," Pashtuns are our brothers sharing the same religion, language, culture and traditions; this land was separated from Afghanistan, and an imposed line was drawn to separate the two brothers.

- However, we want a choice of self-determination for the Pashtuns and Balouches, preserving the territorial integrity of Afghanistan. Therefore, we want to resolve the problem of the Durand Line by peaceful negotiation with Pakistan with the participation of the representatives of Pashtuns and Balouches under the auspices of the United Nations.

- A solid and final determination concerning amnesty or trial of the Afghan war criminals, violators of human rights and national traitors during the past thirty years.

- Searching for practical ways and means for the return of Afghan refugees from Pakistan and Iran and their settlement in uncultivated lands owned by the Government; giving each family a piece of land to build a house; building markets, health clinics, schools, police and security, digging deep wells, installing small diesel generators, building small factories and industries, etc. Under the supervision of the concerned ministry with the help of the world refugee and food organizations and initiating the work program for food.

- Providing settlement for Afghan Nomads (Kouchees) in various parts of the country, considering social justice and their living conditions; selling public lands under favourable terms at affordable prices and long-term payments and also issuing identification documents to the Nomads as a token to quit Nomadism.

- They are finding ways and means to financially support charity institutions such as (Small Islamic Bank) established in California, USA, (War-Torn Children and Ashiana) and the like for creating small industries like handmade items, arts and crafts and other low-priced items.

   Such projects would benefit poverty, unemployment, orphans, widows and maimed persons to make them self-efficient and attract national and international aid.

- Drafting a socio-economic-political and military guideline valid for five years for the future Government of Afghanistan.

- Making a firm decision concerning candidate Afghans who have double Nationality and legalized dual Nationality for all Afghan refugees living in Europe, America, Australia and Elsewhere.

- Revision of the Constitution, if necessary.

- Provisions for the election of the President of the Republic and his two assistants, twenty cabinet members, considering their educational background, practical experience, courage in decision making, righteousness and honesty.

  Selecting Provincial Governors from the 100 members of the "National Inter-Afghan Conference" by direct and secret voting from the three candidates for each position and giving preference to those Government candidates who are citizens of their respective provinces.

  For example, among the three candidates for the Governor of Herat, priority should be given to those who have better education, piety, courage, education, and experience and who are committed to implementing the policies of the central government.

- Finally, all the decisions concerning the election and the articles mentioned above about the functions and duties of the "National Inter-Afghan Conference" would be submitted to "Representative Loya Jirga" for ratification. Members of the "National Inter-Afghan Conference" and the "coordinating committee" will also participate in the "Representative Loya Jirga."

- The First of Jouza 1388 (May 21, 2009) is the termination date of the Presidency of Mr. Karzai. On the completion of the two months emergency, "Representative Loya Jirga" would convene to ratify the decisions of the "National Inter-Afghan Conference." Thus a new chapter would open in the history of Afghanistan.

- After the ratification of the decisions of the "National Inter-Afghan Conference" by "Representative Loya Jirga," the present National Assembly and Senate would be dissolved, except for the members of the cabinet (20) and provincial Governors and twenty Afghan experts for the United Nations.

  Members of the "Representative Loya Jirga" would replace those dissolved for five years; the new President would choose his "Selective Representatives" from the members of the "Inter-Afghan Conference" under article (84), item (3) of the constitution; provincial assemblies each would elect a new chairman.

- At the "Representative Loya Jirga," after the completion of the procedures for ratifying and dissolving during the two months of Hamal and Saour (March 21–May 21), the last day of Mr. Karzai's Presidency is Saour 30th (April 21), under article (61), chapter III of the constitution; on the first day of Djouza 1388 (May 22, 2009) Mr. Karzai will transfer the powers to the new leadership and administration in an official ceremony.

- Mention must be made that from among living abroad, those who are selected to go to Afghanistan as members of the "Representative Loya Jirga" they should serve with righteousness, honesty, responsibility, concern for human rights, love and devotion for Motherland, caring for national interests and not for personal interests.

In addition, they should persuade and encourage other Afghans living abroad to return and serve their country with whatever means available. It is hoped that the Afghan Government or International Institutions will provide for the livelihood of those returning to perform in Afghanistan.

We seek help from Almighty God for success.

LETTER IV

April 18, 2009

E. Fazel Ahmed Afghan
8449 Cambie Street
Vancouver BC V6P 3J9 Canada
His Excellency Mr. Barack H. Obama,
President of the United States, Washington DC

Your Excellency,

I consider it a great honour to say that your strategy for Afghanistan, as recently addressed to the people of the United States and the world, has touched me very much.

Therefore, it is a great honour for me to congratulate Your Excellency. Indeed it is a great pleasure for me to express myself and say that there are some other important issues as well that need to be addressed by your kind administration in cooperation with the future new administration in Kabul, Afghanistan and are outlined as follows:

1. To eliminate the regional crisis, Afghanistan should be recognized as a buffer state between its neighbouring countries. Neither Afghanistan nor a neighbouring country attacks one another, and nor should Afghanistan be used as a means to attack another country.

2. Afghanistan should be recognized as a free, independent and active non-aligned country.

3. Under prevailing conditions and a lack of sufficient military and police forces, Afghanistan cannot adequately combat terrorists and foreign suicide attackers within its borders. Therefore, it would be necessary to allow only a global power under the supervision of the United Nations to remain in Afghanistan for five to six years to assist in this fight.

4. The Afghan national army and police force should be reformed based on former tradition (pre-1978) in the country whereby two years of obligatory national service was required.

5. Appoint an authorized commission composed of experienced Afghan topical experts with the mandate to draft a five-year development plan.

6. Creating a reasonable policy that helps prevent the cultivation, processing and illegal sale and trade of opium.

7. Finding a solution for the problem identified as "Pashtunistan," as Pashtuns are our brothers sharing the same language, culture and traditions. Unfortunately, this land was separated from Afghanistan by force, and an imposed line was drawn to separate the two brothers.

However, today we want a choice of self-determination for the Pashtun and Baloche brothers and sisters, thereby preserving the territorial integrity of Afghanistan. Therefore, we want to resolve the problem of the imposed Durand line through peaceful negotiation with Pakistan, with direct participation from representatives of the governments of Afghanistan and Pakistan along with Pashtun and Baloche representatives, all under the direct auspices of the United Nations.

8. The $1.2 billion a year allocated to Pakistan should be directly spent to support the development of Pashtun and Baloch territories and not for Pakistan's arms and nuclear forces.

9. We Afghans want a strong central government that has complete control over each province.

Therefore, if any financial or technical assistance is extended from a donor country or organization, it should be with the collaboration of the central government, whereby the provincial government is accountable to the central government and the donors for each penny spent.

Thank you for your kind attention, and I would like to take this opportunity to renew to Your Excellency the assurance of my highest consideration.

Yours sincerely,
Engineer Fazel Ahmed Afghan

A Conference for Peace in Afghanistan

Date: Jan 2nd, 2010

Engineer Fazel Ahmed Afghan Hayward,
CA 94536 USA

PEACE PLAN TO EXTINGUISH THE IMPOSED ABLAZE FIRE IN AFGHANISTAN

Dear learned and intellectual fellow Afghans,

I am honoured to be standing here at such a valuable and timely conference with the opportunity to present a plan for peace for our motherland Afghanistan.

Due to time constraints, I do not intend to describe the events of the last 31 years in Afghanistan in detail. However, I only briefly mention that the bloody coup d'etat of April 27, 1978, marked the beginning of the miseries our society has endured over the years, along with the ignition of flames of war that has transformed our motherland into a bloodbath with the bloodshed of her innocent children and created a path of destruction which has flattened clear homes.

Unfortunately, three decades of such pain and suffering have passed. But unfortunately, the flames of such fire have been on the rise due to the continuation of war and terror, with the oppressed people of Afghanistan marching in darkness towards an unknown future.

Eight years ago, with the commencement of the Bonn Conference, the people of Afghanistan had given a glimmer of hope with the establishment of a temporary and transitional government and then an elected President that the people were looking to for a free and prosperous country. But unfortunately, despite all their hopes and dreams, the social, economic, political and national security situations in Afghanistan did not materialize nor stabilize as expected.

Once again, in 2009, the oppressed people of Afghanistan who were counting on transparency in the second term of Presidential elections to find an elected leader and saviour for the nation who could eliminate their miseries and put their country once again on the forgotten path of prosperity were disappointed. They, unfortunately, witnessed the "reappointment" of President Hamid Karzai as the outcome of a shameful election resulting from fraud, corruption and negotiations with foreign powers behind closed doors.

Their hopes and aspirations vanished into thin air with the realization that they would have to live with the same old administration for the next five-year term and that their destiny would be in the hands of foreign sponsors and President Karzai.

The latter would be dining at the same table with an administration that includes certain human rights violators, corrupted warlords and narcotic farmers. In effect, the status quo and the dire situations of the past 30 years prevail.

Dear brothers and sisters, as the brave Afghan nation has moved beyond but not to be forgotten results of the second term Presidential elections with the knowledge or involvement and negative influence of the corrupt and ill-willed as noted above that was the source of creating and imposing an unqualified regime in our dear country, it is now our Islamic, patriotic, national and conscience responsibility as intellectuals to take urgent, positive and effective action to save and bring back our motherland to the once free nation which we inherited from our ancestors.

This sacred dream can only be realized when our patriotic, civil and religious intellectuals who are the anchor of hope for the orphans, widows, disabled, homeless, the ills who live with hunger, poverty and insecurity inside Afghanistan and for those Afghan refugees who live in the camps and slums of Iran and Pakistan take action without prejudice and discrimination. Therefore, for the sake of God and in recognition and honour of the millions of martyrs who lost their lives for our country, our dignity, righteousness and fight for freedom; let's set aside our selfishness, thirst for power, worshiping personalities; and instead I urge you to fill your hearts with the love of patriotism, the worship of God and to work together for the good of our Afghan nation, our neighbours and the world.

This would involve us working in cooperation with severe and honest intent and coming together in unity with the might of an iron fist to identify solutions that would end our country's ongoing crisis.

Working together in a peaceful and productive environment to reach a working resolution and plan that would be proposed as an "Afghan Peace Initiative" at the upcoming International Conference in London and an Inter-Afghan Conference in Kabul.

Such a proposal involving solutions to current issues facing Afghanistan needs to be considered in the context of both domestic and international parameters, with appropriate resolutions being brought forth so that we can, By the will of God and respect for Islamic values, save our homeland from occupation and transform it into a free, independent and prosperous country that supports peace, security and the rule of law.

We, therefore, need to present this "Afghan Peace Initiative" for consideration first at the prospective International Conference to be convened in London this month through the office of the United Nations.

Then, after review and consideration of the proposed plan and in light of the decisions and conclusions of the said International Conference, the proposal should be discussed in an

Inter-Afghan Conference in Kabul before the Grand Assembly (Loya Jirga) proposed by President Karzai, which would include a legitimate group of Afghan representatives but excluding those who have caused bloodshed and been involved with the violation of Human Rights.

Finally, to emerge from the above Afghan conference with decisions and a clear path to save our motherland from the ongoing crisis and create a national government that will bring peace to our beloved nation.

Thereby with your permission, the honourable dignitaries and patriots, brothers and sisters, I would like to share with you my views for your consideration as we set forward today to bring together a peace plan to be discussed at the International as well as at the proposed Inter Afghan Conference:

A. Seven Point Proposal to be tabled at the International Conference in London.

I want to share with you my seven-point proposal first, starting with and discussing President Obama's 3-point strategy on Afghanistan:

1. The deployment of an additional 30,000 American troops would add no further benefit to the current situation but rather be a continuation of irresponsible killings of innocent people and would undermine our Afghan national pride; especially that of our Pashtoon and Baluch brothers and sisters living on both sides of Durand Line.

I, therefore, propose to prioritize the creation of a well-trained instead equipped national army and national police over the next two years. This will coincide with the departure of limited American contingents, as proposed by President Obama, independent of the 70,000 American troops currently in Afghanistan. This is with consideration that the cost incurred for one American trooper is equal to that of 60 Afghan soldiers; in exchange for the additional deployment of 30,000 American troops.

We can train 1,800,000 Afghans to form a national army and the national police that are well equipped. Therefore, while such a significant force for Afghanistan is not needed, it is suggested that the United States spend a quarter of the associated costs of the additional troops, which would prepare a force of approximately 450,000 professionally trained and equipped Afghan army and police personnel to look after the national security, sovereignty and public safety all over the country.

This can indeed happen over the next two to four years before completing President Karzai's term. If such a proposal is implemented, there will be no need for foreign troops to stay beyond four years, and there will be no need to create the already tested destructive militia forces in Afghanistan.

Another benefit of this strategy would be that the United States, by way of reduction of their military expenditures, could invest in the most needed social, economic and military infrastructure of Afghanistan in cooperation with a powerful and centralized Afghan government to gradually develop a society based on genuine democracy and one in line with the social conditions and values of the people of Afghanistan.

To accomplish this strategy, the national army and police will be formed regarding the compulsory military service arrangement that was in place before the bloody coup of April 27, 1978. With this measure in place, the youth from all over our great country, with the support of the whole Nation, can form a unified iron fist to defend the rights, freedom and sovereignty of the country.

To utilize the experiences and dedication of the current and honorary army and police members that may not have the appropriate skills for military and security service, such individuals could be allowed to participate in other proposed organizations of government such as the Public Workforce and Public Green force in the Ministry of Public Works and Ministry of Agriculture with the cooperation of ISAF (the International Security Assistance Force) to accelerate the development of the country.

2. President Obama's plan to direct financial aid to the provinces and local leaders without the accountability of such provincial governments to a powerfully stable and centralized Afghan government, along with the idea of establishing, arming and financially supporting provincial militia forces, needs to be addressed. This not only weakens the central government but would cause a repeat of the bitter and divided experiences the country has faced historically.

Additionally, the pretext of autonomy for the provinces will result in continued warfare that will drag our motherland and her innocent people into unperceivable turmoil.

Therefore, if the foreign powers and President Obama have honest intention to benefit the long-run prosperity of Afghanistan, I present for discussion now and for the proposed Inter-Afghan Conference that instead of offering aid directly to the provinces and local leaders, the United States should implement the proposed fundamental changes that would establish and support a strong central government which in turn would direct and hold accountable the provincial governments and leaders for the benefit and long-run prosperity of the country.

3. President Obama's administration has been increasing aid to the Pakistani government without accepting that Pakistan has continued to use the American government as a cash cow. Pakistan has used a variety of deceptions and excuses to receive substantial funding from the American government. It has indeed used such funding for its interests and against that of American, Afghan and Indian interests.

President Obama has indicated and should follow through as a priority to pressure and hold accountable Pakistan's government to prevent Pakistan's ISI from participating and pursuing its inhumane activities in Afghanistan.

President Obama's Administration has promised aid to Pakistan with the title and intent of crushing the terrorists, particularly al-Qaeda's activities across the border on the so-called Durand Line.

However, the result of such assistance will only lead to the Pakistani government using the funds to wage war against our innocent Pashtoon. Baluch brothers And sisters, including our Afghan immigrant brothers and sisters across the border in Pakistan and with the pretext of dealing with terrorism, will disperse the terrorists like ants all over Afghanistan and neighbouring regions so that they can continue to pursue their inhuman and un-Islamic activities and be a threat to the area and the world.

It is therefore proposed to exert continued and targeted pressure on the Pakistani government and have them commit to a plan to extinguish the ISIs, al-Qaeda's and other terrorist groups' relations with their supporters by cutting off their financial aid and arms.

The US government should no longer present a blank cheque to Pakistan but rather hold them accountable in return for assistance.

As part of exerting pressure and taking a further active role with Pakistan, the United States should target and station a significant portion of the foreign forces in Afghanistan close to the so-called Durand Line, as this is a central source of terrorism.

Additionally, in the International Conference, Afghanistan's neighbouring countries should be strongly encouraged to stay away from destructive interference in Afghanistan's domestic affairs.

They should be further assured that Afghanistan wishes to have peaceful relations with all peace-loving countries and wants to have unique cordial relations with its Islamic and neighbouring countries.

4. Establishing peace in Afghanistan and the region requires the recognition of Afghanistan as a buffer state among its neighbouring countries with the resolution that Afghanistan wouldn't invade any neighbouring country, nor would neighbouring, or foreign countries invade Afghanistan nor use its soil as a platform to attack other countries.

5. One of the key justifications for foreign troops' existence and mission in Afghanistan is to combat terrorism. Therefore it is proposed that the term "terrorism" be defined in the International Conference following International law to clarify the actions that would fall under terrorism.

After that, within the said definition, the Afghan National Army and Police, along with foreign forces, can jointly carry on their legitimate duties of fighting terrorism without killing innocent people or destroying their homes. This is crucial to shed light and provide direction on a critical mission and one that would allow targeted focus on the areas that pose such a threat.

6. The following outlines another point that would support our sovereignty and ability to operate under the Afghan rule of law effectively. I propose that all foreign prisons in Afghanistan be shut down orderly. Instead, all Afghan prisoners are transferred to Afghan-controlled prisons together with their records so that their cases can be reviewed and evaluated by Afghan courts of law.

7. Lastly, as noted, it is vital that, in addition to the International Conference in London, such matters be proposed and discussed with the key stakeholders in Afghanistan via a proposed Inter-Afghan Conference.

It should be agreed and ratified that such a conference involve and be open to legitimate representatives of all political parties, including opposing President Karzai's administration. It is also essential that a cease-fire be implemented before the said Conference to establish a venue of open dialogue, cooperation and peace.

The Afghan government should collaborate with and support the UN representative in Kabul to establish such a conference and ensure the logistical and security arrangements are made to allow for a peaceful and productive dialogue.

B. Proposal to be discussed at an Inter Afghan Conference

My fellow Afghans, we are all directly or indirectly aware of the proceedings and downturn of the past eight years in our country, along with the presidential election of Aug. 20th, 2009, which involved negotiations with foreign powers behind closed doors.

Accordingly, I believe that the current dire situation is not a solution to our problems and, if continued, will carry devastating consequences that may not be rectifiable. If the government's opposition is under the belief that ongoing war and killings will be the pathway to peace, they are seriously mistaken.

Some people believe that the calling of the traditional National Grand Assembly (Loya Jirga), which makes crucial and strategic decisions concerning national issues at present, is the solution for today's crisis and one that would defuse the flames engulfing our country.

Here, I should remind you that due to the demise of our national unity over the past three decades, the Grand Assembly (Loya Jirga), as once intended, would not operate effectively under current circumstances but rather operate in the same "ceremonial" manner as the Grand Assembly that resulted in the appointment of President Hamid Karzai as the President of the Transitional Government of Afghanistan.

Therefore, under the dire prevailing situations as the oppressed nation and the patriotic scholars, in particular, are set forth to an essential and historic task; we need to ensure that the direction we take is in line and complies with the provisions of our constitution as adopted by President Karzai's government as well as supported by the international community.

Therefore, I set forth for your consideration the following proposal for fundamental changes in the government of Afghanistan, which is following the terms of our constitution.

While it may be difficult to swallow and like drinking a glass of poison to accept the legitimacy of President Karzai's recent election; under the current challenging and fragile situation our country is facing, we should be open to receiving President Karzai up until the calling of the Grand Assembly (Loya Jirga) in two years as proposed by President Karzai. This will also coincide with the commencement of the departure of American troops, as indicated by President Obama.

Furthermore, we should make such a compromise and adopt an inclusive policy that allows for negotiation with the government's opposition and also opens the door for the participation of their legitimate delegates in the proposed Interim Afghan Conference to enable us to find practical ways to establish peace for a prosperous and free Afghanistan.

Also, by submission of the above plan, we can convince the intervening international forces at the International Conference that the continuation of war under different names is not the solution.

So we had better jointly seek ways to get out of the deadlock and prepare grounds for the gradual and dignified departure of all foreign troops within the next four years, based on a departure schedule accepted by the Afghan government and the world.

This way, we can jointly attempt to create a relatively national government, free of today's administrative corruption, for an independent, free and non-allied country which can be a friend and suitable partner with the international community. This can materialize from the beginning of the second round term of President Karzai, which comprises a two-year transitional period or maybe a full five-year term in office.

This dream will only be realized if the loose thread currently connecting President Karzai with the international forces is kept intact. But unfortunately, such a fragile tie could be cut off at any time due to conflicts between the Afghan and international governments.

Our hopes for a more robust and peaceful Afghanistan can only come true if we stabilize this thread by bringing together several virtuous, honest and patriotic Afghan scholars to liaise in the middle of such a line for the above-mentioned two-year transition period. This will allow them to strengthen and take control of the fragile situation and be in the best position to negotiate with the respective parties about any possible resolutions relating to the elimination of the current crisis and the creation of a promising future for Afghanistan.

Another critical goal over the said two-year transition period would be the integration of all currently registered parties and the creation of two representative national political parties that would start working towards inclusive participation in the prospective national Grand Assembly (Loya Jirga) and the creation of a proper federal government.

For the success of this grand objective, it is necessary to open the door for negotiations with the government's opposition, including leaders of the opposition such as Mr. Golbaddin Hekmatyar, Mr. Jalalluddin Haqani and Mr. Mulla Mohammad Omer, with the understanding that war is not the solution for peace and freedom in Afghanistan.

Therefore, these opposition leaders should be invited to introduce their authorized representatives to participate in the proposed Inter-Afghan conference to be convened in Kabul with the commitment that a ceasefire must be adopted during such time to allow for productive and peaceful discussions.

Therefore, I suggest the appointment of a delegation consisting of the following individuals be commissioned to meet with the opposition leaders at their earliest convenience and at a mutually agreed-upon venue to invite the opposition to introduce their virtuous and patriotic representatives whose hands are not stained with the blood of Afghans:

My suggested delegation of respected individuals to negotiate with the opposition leaders is as follows:

1. Mr. Seyed Ahmad Gilani

2. Dr. Abdulsattar Sirat

3. Dr. Farough Aazam

4. Mr. Seyed Jalal Karim

5. Mr. Golagha Shiroozi

6. Mr. Mohtasebollah Mazhabi

With your permission, the following will set out the essential points about the proposal for fundamental changes to be discussed at the proposed Inter-Afghan conference to be convened according to the International Conference in London with the hopes of establishing peace and prosperity in our adored motherland.

Firstly, according to the resolutions and agreements reached by the International Conference and in line with the terms of item 20 of section 64 from chapter four of our Constitution; His Excellency, President Hamid Karzai, the President of the Islamic government of Afghanistan, ordered the Elections Commission to establish the following two commissions in Kabul:

1. The High Executive and Parliamentary Council

2. The High Council of the Professionals and the Auditor General

3. The High Executive and Parliamentary Council.

Such a Council would comprise approximately 400 intellectual Afghans living inside and or outside of the country who have no criminal records and haven't been implicated in any violation of human rights. This Council would be established under item 5, section 158 of chapter 12 of the Constitution and its members be elected or appointed as outlined in the following section under the supervision of the Elections Commission and UN representatives: Members of High Executive and Parliamentary Council

1. All members of the Bonn Conference, representing the Rome Conference, Peshawar Conference, Cypress Conference, Afghan Mellat, and the Northern United Front, will be included.

2. President, two vice presidents and two secretaries of Parliament.

3. Thirty-four members from Parliament for representation of thirty-four provinces...

4. President, two vice presidents and two secretaries of the Senate.

5. Thirty-four members from the Senate for representation of thirty-four provinces.

6. Ten representatives from the Taliban movement.

7. Ten representatives from the Islamic Party of Mr. G. Hekmatyar.

8. Ten representatives from the "People's Democratic Party, later called Watan," including five from Parcham and five from Khalq.

9. Ten representatives from Jalaluddin Haqqani Party.

10. Sixty representatives from the faculty members of Universities throughout Afghanistan.

11. Eight representatives from various non-aligned and nonpartisan InterAfghan conferences held in America, Europe and Australia during the last several years.

12. Seventy people from Afghan Technocrats were included in the United Nations list issued in 1993/1994.

13. All 34 Chairs of the Provincial Councils throughout Afghanistan. The Council will be established to pursue the following mandate:

- Establishment of peace, national unity and national compromise for a free, independent, united and sovereign Afghanistan,
- Establishment of the rule of law, equity and equality of women and men and justice to develop and strengthen the present system,
- Formation of a self-sufficient national army and police to defend the federal and territorial sovereignty of the country and maintain peace in the country,
- Gradual development and promotion of democracy in line with the view of the country's social climate and values,

- Laying the foundation for the formation of two representative national political parties,
- Promoting the establishment of cooperation and coordination among the three branches of the State,
- Serious cooperation with the High Council of Experts and Professionals and with the Auditor General to champion professional and expert standards across all areas of government operations,
- Uprooting fraud in the administration,
- Development of equal education with high standards in consideration of Afghan culture for all Afghans,
- Establishing and encouraging cordial relations with all peace-loving nations of the world,
- Advocating the fight to eradicate the roots of terrorism in the country, and
- Creation of strong and healthy Executive and Parliamentary branches of the state acceptable to the Afghan and international communities.

Appropriate efforts must be made so that without prejudice and hostile intentions, the clergy, scholars, distinguished citizens, representatives of the opposition, members of the national parliament, technocrats, provincial representatives and presidential candidates be chosen to exhibit national representation and one that is viewed positively internationally.

The following is a brief description of the start-up procedures for the High Executive and Parliamentary Counsel, which will later transition into two separate organizations forming the Executive and the Parliamentary branches of the state:

A. The High Council should initially convene with consideration of Islamic and Afghan traditions and with the interim chairmanship of the Special Representative of the General Secretary of the United Nations. Immediately after that, a virtuous, learned, experienced and patriotic person with a postgraduate degree should be elected as the High Council chair replacing the interim chair through a direct, free and confidential vote.

B. The council shall then, under the direction of the Council Chair utilizing a direct, free and confidential ballot elect a deputy and two secretaries from candidates that have virtue, who are learned, patriotic, experienced and hold a postgraduate degree.

1. Description of Duties for the High Executive and Parliamentary Council

Due to time constraints, I would like to share with you a summary and focal points of their duties as follows:

Effective execution of the above proposals requires an effective, qualified, working and honest Executive Council that can be trusted by the Afghan people and by the broader international community.

Therefore, it is necessary that the virtuous Afghans and the dynamic international forces who are engaged in Afghanistan and who wish to realize national unity, peace, compromise, an extinguishment of fraud and terrorism, the rule of law, equal rights and true democracy in Afghanistan to raise their voice in a friendly and respectful manner and ask the first and second vice presidents to submit their resignation to His Excellency President Hamid Karzai for the sake of God, national peace, compromise and in the utmost interest of the oppressed people of Afghanistan.

Next, for President Karzai to accept their resignation in line with allowable rules of our constitution in line with item number ten, section Sixty-four of chapter three of the constitution allow the High Executive and Parliamentary Council to elect two qualified patriotic persons of virtue and honour, holding a postgraduate degree and who believe in a stable and efficient central government through a free, direct and confidential ballot and to introduce them to the president for appointment.

Consequent to the said appointments by the President, one of the appointees will be assigned the First Vice President and chair of the Executive Branch and the other as the Second Vice President and chair of the High Council of the Experts/Professionals in the Department of the Auditor General. After the appointment of the vice presidents, the cabinet of President Karzai for the well-being of the nation should resign so that the High Executive and Parliamentary Council can choose and appoint new members of the cabinet that are virtuous, learned, experienced, professional, highly educated and patriotic from within members of the High Executive and Parliamentary Council and from the resigned members of President Hamid Karzai's cabinet and then subsequently introduce them to President Karzai for appointment under item number 11, section 64 of chapter three of Afghanistan's constitution.

After that, 34 people may include members of the High Executive and Parliamentary Counsel and the resigned members of the cabinet who are also highly educated, experienced, honest, patriotic, of good reputation amongst the people and true believers in the benefits of a strong central government should be elected and introduced to President Karzai appointed as the governors of the provinces under item number 13, section 64 of chapter four of the constitution.

Further, two deputies from the members of the High Executive and Parliamentary Counsel should be elected by free, direct and secret ballot and be introduced by the Second Vice President to President Karzai as deputies for the High Council of the Experts/Professionals and the High Council of the Auditor General.

While Sections 83 and 84 of chapter five of the constitution explicitly state that the parliament and senate elections include one person from each district council and that the polls from the provinces and districts be based on the proportionate population of each province and district.

However, due to the lack of security, a national census and citizenship certification, all of which are required to hold such elections, district council elections have not been held.

Therefore, due to the nonexistence of such district elections, the due process for the parliament and senate elections has not been carried out, making the first round and upcoming national assembly unlawful and in contradiction to the constitution's requirements.

Accordingly, it is proposed that until the restoration of security is restored across the country to allow for completion of a census, issuance of citizenship cards and district council elections that the national assembly elections be postponed and alternatively temporarily substituted by the creation of the 400-member High Executive and Parliamentary Council consisting of the Executive Council (two vice presidents, cabinet, provincial governors and deputies of the Experts Council and the Auditor General) and Parliamentary council which would consist of the remaining 400 members and act as the interim parliament.

This interim parliament shall, after having chosen its chair, deputies and secretaries through a free, direct and secret ballot under section 156, chapter 11 of the constitution, under the supervision of the elections commission and by the presidential decree, assume the role of the national assembly during the two-year transition period up until the next official elections for the national assembly

2. The High Council of Experts, Professionals and the Auditor General

The leading organizations of the Experts and the Auditor General, known as the Chief of the Experts and Chief of the Department of the Auditor General, will incorporate a joint high-level board under the chairmanship of the second vice president. However, they shall operate separately within their charter and due regulations.

A. The Chief General/Chairman of the Experts/Professionals

The Chief General of the Experts/Professionals should comprise Afghan and international skilled professionals in technology, engineering, finance, planning, education, arts and other critical social, economic, political and military services. Furthermore, under its constitution and due regulations, it should cooperate with the three branches of the state and the Chief Auditor General to provide the necessary skills, expertise and guidance to improve the level of quality and efficiency in the operations of the government.

B. The Chief General/Chairman of the Department of the Auditor General

The Chief General of the Auditor General's office should comprise of honest, virtuous, learned and patriotic individuals with knowledge of accounting, finance and administration, which should work together and cooperate with the three branches of the state and the Chief General of the Experts at the federal level and with the regional, provincial levels as well to aid accountability, improve the administration's financial systems and to establish a high quality, modern, accountable and transparent administration, free of corruption and that can be trusted by the Afghan nation and the international community.

As I conclude, with great hopes, I wish for success for this Afghan Conference to discuss and find a path for peace for our motherland. I want to emphasize that no one can rebuild our destroyed country except for the wise, learned, virtuous and patriotic Afghans and thus, it is in our hands to take on this critical task. I also sincerely hope this won't be the last conference of this type and that its resolutions will not be shelved or ignored but seriously pursued by a central and robust organization of the learned, and one that continues to keep our Afghan brothers and sisters updated on the progress and activities of such an organization. With the success and efforts of this gathering,

I propose that a strong central committee consisting of our dear fellow Afghans who have initiated this conference at Hayward, California, establish a branch office in Kabul and other areas of the world where Afghans reside and continue their outstanding efforts and commitments for peace and to promote prosperity, sovereignty and freedom for our motherland at the national and international levels through peaceful relations. Finally, I hope our learned and distinguished Afghans act in the same way as the sunshine that views our Afghan brothers and sisters equally with one eye and like the moon that throws light at every darkness of our adored motherland Afghanistan; so that with the mercy of God, the Afghan nation will no longer be a burden on the shoulders of others and that our government will rise from the rubbles of war, rebuild the country with its own hands and stand up for its rights. I want to end by wishing everyone a happy New Year and hope for peace and prosperity for all nations, including our beloved motherland Afghanistan.

God bless all.

LETTER V

Engineer Fazel Ahmed Afghan

8449 Cambie St.
Vancouver BC, V6P 3J9
Home Tel: 604 325 5271
Cell Tel: 604 561 9401
E-Mail: afghanfazel@hotmail.com

Dear and Respected Friends,

Since this is the last year of President Obama's second term, I would like to draw your kind attention to my proposal to Mr. Obama, which I sent just before he became the President of the United States. It was under the title "Fundamental Changes in the Government of Afghanistan. Engineer Fazel Ahmed Afghan, Dec 20th, 2008.

As is known to everybody, the slogan of President Obama during the campaign was "Change." Of course, the purpose of the motto of change was not merely the changing of a white President to a black President. Still, his sincere desire was to introduce fundamental changes in the scattered socioeconomic, political and military status of America at the national and international levels so that he could introduce rapid and all-sided developments. It was meant not only to regain the prestige of the United States of America throughout the world but elevate it as well.

In other words, the slogan of change which reflects Mr. Barack Obama's sacred national goals made him a beloved leader to both white and black Americans. It enabled him to become the leader of the most powerful nation on Earth and to govern this nation. Indeed, the American nation, by electing Mr. Obama, proved to the world that their national interests are higher than colour, minority and majority. It showed that purity, sincerity, honesty, knowledge, patriotism and broadmindedness are qualities which constitute the character of Mr. Obama and gained him success in the election at both national and international levels.

In addition, he stood free of the old and unpopular contradictions and forgotten inhuman values. Unfortunately, the oppressed nation of Afghan would, once again, face a vital national trial. Contrary to what we observed in the American election, several unworthy personas are planning to hold an election using slogans of ethnic, religious and regional phrases and cheating people by misinterpreting the articles of the constitution.

Their goal is to collect votes from illiterate, uninformed and ignorant people to establish themselves as winners. This is happening at a time when the national infrastructure is being destroyed. The nation is fighting an imposed war, the census has not been taken, local consultative assemblies have not been established, security does not exist, millions of refugees are still abroad, corruption, bribery, and injustice prevail, and Afghan culture is under foreign domination.

There is no law and order in the country. There is no unity between the house and the senate, and the election commission has significant differences between the President of the Republic and the home. Irresponsible attacks of foreign forces continue on the defenceless villages and towns, and suicidal attacks kill many innocent people. Mr. Karzai is fighting with the united front, and heroin production and its illegal trade continue as before.

This unworthy governing group cares only for its interests, stamping the national interests; they do not believe in social equality, human dignity, human rights, piety, sincerity, honesty and patriotism. They are struggling merely for power and money, cheating uninformed and ignorant people.

In recognition of the above problems and the fact that the destiny of the oppressed Afghan nation has been determined from abroad during the past thirty years. The national social code by which the government resolved its national problems by convening the traditional great national assembly (Loya Jirga) is no longer feasible. The nation at this time cannot determine its destiny, nor can the foreign powers impose their will on the Afghan government. It is therefore essential that the Afghan nation, especially the Afghan intellectual group, those with piety, honesty, patriotism and experience, who have not stampeded human rights and enjoy the trust of the United Nations, should take the initiative to implement the "Proposal for the Fundamental Changes in the Government of Afghanistan."

Taking into consideration the internal and regional conditions included in the proposal. It is emphasized that the views and findings of the United Nations mission consisting of 15 members, including the big powers, such as the USA, Russian Federation and the People's Republic of China, which has recently visited Afghanistan, should also be considered.

It is expected that the mission has touched on the realities and the numerous problems Afghanistan has been facing during the past thirty years, as well as the foreign interferences in Afghanistan.

Before making a quick conclusion and decision, the mission should read the "Proposal for Fundamental Changes in the Government of Afghanistan," which suggests the convening of a national winter afghan conference and the Afghan representative national (Loya Jirga).

Then after the approval of the security council, it submits recommendations to the Karzi government and the coordinating committee of the inter-Afghan conference. Mr.Hamed Karzai, The President of the Islamic Republic of Afghanistan, too, considers his conscious, moral, religious, Islamic and international obligations to protect his honour and the salvation of the motherland. A country which he has inherited from his ancestors and which cannot tolerate misery and maltreatment anymore.

He should accept that the forthcoming election based on the constitution is improper, unjust and in contradiction with the social justice, national interest of the country and the world's opinion. It is therefore respectfully suggested that a different way should be sought, which is the "Proposal for Fundamental Changes in the Government of Afghanistan," by the implementation of which the oppressed Afghan nation, as well as the entire world, would enjoy peace and comfort during the forthcoming years. In other words, based on article (64), item chapter III of the constitution concerning (the Presidency) and chapter IX about (emergency), the President, after the approval of the national assembly, should declare a crisis in the country due to the reason of dominant insecurity, terrorism and suicidal attacks in many parts of the country.

Therefore, he should demand from the United Nations the convening of the Inter-Afghan National Conference, as well as the Great National Representative Assembly (Loya Jirga).

A: Proposed "Representative Loya Jirga"

1. Under the current challenging conditions, the traditional (Loya Jirga) cannot be convened; therefore, it is necessary to demand the moral and financial cooperation of the United Nations to invite and convene an Inter-Afghan Conference consisting of 400 Afghan patriotic scholars and intellectuals whose names have not been listed as violators of human rights.

They would relatively represent the Afghan societies in and out of Afghanistan as a substitute for the traditional Loya Jirga. So-called (Representative Loya Jirga) This group of 400 should then elect a group of highly educated and respected 100 Afghans by free, direct and secret voting from among themselves, supervised by a Non-Afghan institution, trustworthy and acceptable to Afghans.

The Non-Afghan institution would lead and execute the election using a computer-based method. The elected group of 100 would form and convene the "Inter-Afghan Conference."

Further details in this connection follow:

2. It may be advisable if the United Nations select 20 neutral and non-aligned Afghan scholars by direct and secret computerized voting, performed by a NonAfghan institution trusted and approved by Afghans, to participate in the proposed 400 members "Representative Loya Jirga."

Then six persons from these 20 persons will be selected by a similar computerized system to participate in the 100-member "InterAfghan Conference," held in Kabul, the capital of Afghanistan. The selected six persons will be then introduced to the special envoy of the United Nations as members of the "coordinating committee" of the 100 members ``Inter-Afghan National Conference" so that under the United Nations auspices and financial aid, members of the proposed "Representatives Loya Jirga," consisting of scholars and intellectuals are selected to begin their task force. Members of the "coordinating committee" have equal rights and privileges of voting and candidacy like other members of the proposed "InterAfghan Conference" and "Representative Loya Jirga."

The number of the members of the proposed "Representative Loya Jirga," including the members of the "coordinating committee" and"Inter-Afghan Conference," are introduced to be included as follows:

3. All the members of the Bonn Conference, representing the Rome Conference, Peshawar Conference, Cypress Conference and the Northern United Front.

4. The President of the National Assembly, his two assistants and the two secretaries of the National Assembly, and 25 members of the National assembly.

5. The President of the Senate, his two assistants and the two secretaries, together with ten members of the Senate.

6. Presidents of the Provincial Assemblies.

7. Ten persons representing the Taliban movement.

8. Ten persons are represented by the Islamic Party of Hekmatyar.

9. Ten persons representing the "Peoples Democratic Party," five from "The Khalq faction," and five from "The Parcham faction."

10. Ten persons representing the "Jalaluddin Haqqani Party."

11. Twenty persons representing the current Government Executive and Judiciary sections.

12. Sixty persons representing various Universities of Afghanistan. The Ministry of Higher Education will determine the number of each University about the number of the Academic boards of each University.

13. Eighty persons representing various non-aligned and nonpartisan InterAfghan conferences held in America and Europe during the past seven years (the number of shares of each meeting will be determined by the number of participants in each conference).

14. Finally, about seventy persons representing the Afghan Technocrats were included in the United Nations lists of 1993 and 1994.

B: Duties of the Proposed "Representative Loya Jirga"

1. Selecting the members of the "Inter-Afghan Conference."

2. Ratifying the resolutions of the "National Inter-Afghan Conference."

3. With the exclusion of seventy-six persons (detailed in the duties of the "National Inter-Afghan Conference"), extending the existence and authorities of the current National Assembly and the Senate of Afghanistan for five years.

C: Duties and Functions of the Proposed "National Inter-Afghan Conference":

The National Inter-Afghan Conference will be held in Kabul under a temporary Chairmanship of the special envoy of the United Nations, observing a special Islamic ceremony and will perform the following duties after the approval of the plan and procedure of the Conference.

1. Electing the President and two secretaries of the Inter-Afghan Conference by free and secret voting among three candidates.

2. Approving the Agenda and procedure of the Conference.

3. Discussing and making decisions on the following proposals.

i. To eliminate the regional crisis, Afghanistan should be recognized as a buffer state between the neighbouring countries. So that neither Afghanistan attacks another country nor another country attacks Afghanistan, and Afghanistan should not be used as a means to attack another country.

ii. Afghanistan should be recognized as a free, independent and non-aligned country, active and not indifferent.

iii. Whereas under the prevailing conditions, due to the lacking of sufficient military and police forces, Afghanistan cannot fight the terrorists and foreign suicidal attackers. Therefore, it would be necessary to allow only an international force under the supervision of the United Nations to remain in Afghanistan for five-six years to fight the terrorists jointly under a bipartisan agreement with the Afghan National Army; such an experience would also train and equip the Afghan Army for the future of the Country.

iv. Afghan National Army and Police should be reformed based on the former (1978) tradition of two years of "National Obligatory Service."

v. Whereas security and stability are essential for implementing socio-economic-political programs. Therefore severe measures should be adopted to collect arms from armed civilians, as well as from (NGOs"s) and warlords.

The Government should declare and warn that all forms of arms, excluding small pistols and hunting guns, must be returned to the Government free of cost or in exchange for food, clothing, agricultural seeds, fertilizers or industrial tools; otherwise, the Government would use force to collect the arms from the public and those not cooperating would be punished.

In Kabul as well as other cities, arms should be collected from all civilians, warlords, Afghan and Non-Afghan institutions and NGO'sThe security of the towns, Government organizations, private institutions, foreign Embassies, Consulates, and commercial agencies should be guaranteed by the joint U.N. and Afghan forces based on bilateral agreements. Parties not accepting the Government order should be seriously punished.

vi.   Appointing an authorized commission among experienced Afghan experts to draft five- five years developmental plans for 25 years with the cooperation of foreign experts.

Considering the socioeconomic-military and human resources conditions of the country and the priorities. This plan should be prepared within six to nine months to be submitted to foreign investors and international institutions to attract foreign financial and technical aid to reconstruct Afghanistan's infrastructure.

vii.   Appointing twenty scholars consisting of economic, military, social and political experts by free and secret voting from the members of the "Inter-Afghan National Conference" to be stationed at the United Nations in New York for five years. They will function as a bridge and liaison between the United Nations and the Government of Afghanistan for coordinating various functions.

viii.   Gradual coordination of the implementation of the process of democracy and the free market with the process of socioeconomic development and law enforcement in all Government and private sectors; searching for ways and means to attract and encourage the participation of Afghan societies in Government affairs, projects and in the process of reconstruction in particular.

ix.   Accepting the theory of creating government cooperatives to compete with the internal and external private sectors in matters such as the supply of food (i.e. tea, sugar, edible oil, benzine, gas, flour, and wheat) and reorganizing the old system of distributing "Coupons" to the Government employees, teachers, contract employees and military officers.

x.   Creating a reasonable policy for avoiding the cultivation, processing and illegal sale and trade of opium; creating work and employment for the peasants engaged in such matters; tracing and punishing internal and foreign heroin dealers; implementing heavy punishments like those in Saudi Arabia on the dealers; encouraging landowners to cultivate such substitute as saffron, cotton, sugar cane, beetroot, horticulture, raising livestock, poultry, ice-making factories in the main cities and simple ones in the villages; using solar energy and small generators for creating energy; giving long-term loans for the realization of those projects: establishing agricultural cooperatives and small factories for processing food items, fruits, candies and the like.

xi.   Researching on the claims of Afghanistan and the Russian Federation in connection to the former demand for the war compensation/reparation and the latter demand for the payment of the loans given to former puppet Governments and reaching a final solution under the auspices of the security council.

xii.   Finding a solution to the problem of "Pashtunistan," Pashtuns are our brothers sharing the same religion, language, culture and traditions; this land was separated from Afghanistan, and an imposed line was drawn to separate the two brothers.

However, we want today a choice of self-determination for the Pashtuns and Balouches, preserving the territorial integrity of Afghanistan. We want to resolve the problem of the Durand Line by peaceful negotiation with Pakistan with the participation of the representatives of Pashtuns and Balouches under the auspices of the United Nations.

xiii.   A solid and final determination concerning amnesty or trial of the Afghan war criminals, violators of human rights and national traitors during the past thirty years.

xiv.   Searching for practical ways and means for the return of Afghan refugees from Pakistan and Iran and their settlement in uncultivated lands owned by the Government; giving each family a piece of land to build a house; building markets, health clinics, schools, police and security, digging deep wells, installing small diesel generators, building small factories and industries, etc.

Under the supervision of the concerned ministry with the help of the world refugee and food organizations and initiating the program of work for food.

xv.   Providing settlement for Afghan Nomads (Kouchees) in various parts of the country, considering social justice and their living conditions; selling public lands under favourable terms at affordable prices and long-term payments and issuing identification documents to the Nomads as a token to quit Nomadism.

xvi.   Finding ways and means to financially support charity institutions such as (Small Islamic Bank) established in California, USA, (War-Torn Children and Ashiana) and the like for creating small industries like handmade items, arts and crafts and other low-priced items.

Such projects would benefit poverty, unemployment, orphans, widows and maimed persons to make them self-efficient and would attract national and international aid. (xvii) Drafting a socio-economic-political and military guideline valid for five years for the future Government of Afghanistan.

xvii.   Making a firm decision concerning candidate Afghans who have double Nationality and legalization of dual Nationality for all Afghan refugees living in Europe, America, Australia and Elsewhere.

xviii.   Revision of the Constitution, if necessary. (xx) Provisions for the election of the President of the Republic and his two assistants, twenty members of the cabinet, considering their educational background, practical experience, courage in decision making, piety and honesty. Selecting Provincial Governors from the 100 members of the "National InterAfghan Conference" by direct and secret voting from the three candidates for each position.

Giving preference to those Government candidates who are citizens of their respective provinces. For example, among the three candidates for the Governor of Herat, priority should be given to those who have better education, piety, courage, education, experienced and who are committed to implementing the policies of the central Government.

xix.   Finally, all the decisions concerning the election and all the articles mentioned earlier about the functions and duties of the "National Inter-Afghan Conference" would be submitted to "Representative Loya Jirga" for ratification. Members of the "National Inter-Afghan Conference" and the "coordinating committee" will also participate in the "Representative Loya Jirga."

xx.   The First of Jouza 1388 (May 21, 2009) is the termination date of the Presidency of Mr. Karzai. On the completion of the two months emergency, "Representative Loya Jirga" would convene to ratify the decisions of the "National Inter-Afghan Conference." Thus a new chapter would open in the history of Afghanistan.

xxi.   After the ratification of the decisions of the "National InterAfghan Conference" by "Representative Loya Jirga," the present National Assembly and Senate would be dissolved, except for the members of the cabinet (20) and provincial Governors and twenty Afghan experts for the United Nations. Members of the "Representative Loya Jirga" would replace those dissolved for five years; the new President would choose his "Selective Representatives" from the members of the "Inter-Afghan Conference" under article (84), item (3) of the constitution; provincial assemblies each would elect a new chairman.

xxii.   At the "Representative Loya Jirga," after the completion of the procedures for ratifying and dissolving during the two months of Hamal and Saour (March 21st - May 21st), the last day of Mr. Karzai's Presidency is Saour 30th (April 21st), under article (61), chapter III of the constitution; on the first day of Djouza 1388 (May 22, 2009) Mr. Karzai will transfer the powers to the new leadership and administration in an official ceremony.

xxiii.   Mention must be made that from among living abroad, those who are selected to go to Afghanistan as members of the "Representative Loya Jirga" they should serve with piety, honesty, responsibility, concern for human rights, love and devotion for Motherland, caring for national interests and not for personal interests;

In addition, they should persuade and encourage other Afghans living abroad to return and serve their country with whatever means available. It is hoped that the Afghan Government or International Institutions will provide for the livelihood of those returning to serve in Afghanistan.

We seek help from Almighty God for success.

LETTER VI

Fazel Ahmed Afghan.
#402-538 W 45th Ave
Vancouver, BC Canada
The United States 21/02/2021
Institute of Peace

The Afghanistan Study Group.

To: All Honorable.
-Senator Kelly A. Ayotte.
-General Joseph F. Dunford, Jr.
-Honorable Nancy Lindborg.

Peace Proposal for Afghanistan.

I read your Final ASG Report and listened to the prepared Video; I was impressed. Therefore from the bottom of my heart congratulate you for the excellent and profound analysis of the situation in Afghanistan, especially in the last 19 years.

Unfortunately, in the last 19 years, much precious life of American, NATO and Afghan Soldiers were lost in unjustified imposed War under different names such as Alqa-e-Dah, Taliban, Hikmatyar, Haqqani and ISIS groups armed and trained in Pakistan; I mean all these criminal groups have been other Vehicles, stationed in Pakistan.

The steering wheel and the accelerator pedal are under the control of the Pakistani military (ISI). What I am trying to say is that the Pakistani Military has to be convinced to stop interference in Afghan and Taliban peace negotiations and cooperate to bring peace to Afghanistan and the region. Otherwise, peace will be impossible; as a result, there will be civil war.

The country will go back to before 2001; as a result, all the efforts of the US and NATO to bring peace and democracy to Afghanistan will go down the drain. So it would be a disaster not only for the people of Afghanistan and the region, it would be a big celebration for all US adversaries in the area. Pakistan and Russia have forced the Taliban to say that they will negotiate peace when Dr. Ashraf Ghani resigns and forms a transitional Government like after the Bonn conference in 2001.

To those who want a transitory government like after the Bonn conference, I would like to say they again dream of turning back Afghanistan to disasters and dark Eras in 80th and 90th of 20th century, that is unconstitutional because the Bonn conference was held because, in Mujahideen and Taliban Eras in Afghanistan, there was no any constitution and law and order in the country

Therefore, the Bonn conference decided to form a transitional government to make a constitution approved by a grand assembly and then have a fair and free election that all the people of Afghanistan can express their well and choose the president to form a government that all can see themselves in it. Now we have one of the best constitutions in the region. Therefore we can not go back to Mujahideen and Taliban dark Eras and once again destroy what we have achieved in the last 19 years.

Therefore I humbly submit. My proposal to respected members of ASG is as follows.

1. Convince Pakistan to let Afghanistan have a peaceful democratic government in SAR. For God's sake, let the Afghan Nation have peace and move to prosperity and have peaceful, friendly and cordial relations with Pakistan, the region and the whole world.

2. Though Dr. Ashraf Ghani is a very knowledgeable genius, he is not a corrupted person. He is doing his best for the country and democracy. Still, unfortunately, due to the interferences of the countries in neighbour as well the presence of notorious internal warlords, the Government under the leadership of Dr. Ashraf Ghani is not functioning well; therefore, he should accept that his honest efforts under the present situation not workable and the US adversaries in the region, is trying to take the country to a civil war and what has been achieved in 19 years will go down in the drain. Therefore, I humbly make the following proposals.

A- Dr. Ashraf Ghani, the elected president of Afghanistan, should call a Grand advisory assembly comprising of 4000 representatives from government, nongovernment, Taliban, and all appositions to be selected in a free and fair election from all provinces and district governments of the country to assemble in specific date in Kabul city to decide.

1. To agree on the primary objectives (Guideline) of a new constitution for a new government,

2. Electing a commission of 50 or more people from the grand assembly in a free and fair election to bring changes in the present constitution acceptable to all.

3. After making the new constitution based on the main guideline and preserving democracy and all achievements in the last 19 years in a united sovereign and independent country.

4. The new constitution should be submitted to the Grand assembly for approval.

5. After the approval of the new constitution, Dr. Ashraf Ghani should resign, and in three months, the presidential election should be held in a free and fair election. None of the above would be achieved without a total ceasefire

Therefore, first, both sides should agree on a complete ceasefire in the country, then an election for the Grand assembly would be held in a peaceful environment in the country. b- The presence of US and NATO forces in Afghanistan.

Because the Taliban, Pakistan, ISIS and some warlords in the country oppose the presence of foreign troops under the US and NATO, I propose both forces should join under the name of the United Nations Peacekeeping force for two years.

After two years, if the US and NATO feel like staying and having a base under the same conditions they have in Germany and Japan for a longer time to keep peace in South Asia and the region, I am sure the future government, after the approval of the Grand Assemble, would sign a treaty with NATO.

Sincerely yours.
Engineer Fazel Ahmed Afghan.

Cc:
-Honorable.
General Secretary, United Nations.
United Nations Secretariat
New York.
N.Y.10017
usa@un.int uk@un.int
indiaun@prodigy.net
turkey@un.int CONS
Engineer Fazel Ahmed Afghan, MSc
Canada:- Sept 11, 2016

My Sad Memory from the Tragedy of September 11, 2001, 2001

After nine months of President George W. Bush in power, on September 9th, 2001, Ahmed Shah Masud was assassinated in Khwaja Bahauddin, Taloqan, Afghanistan; that puzzle wasn't solved yet. It was 7:00 a.m. in Vancouver, B.C. Canada, which was 10:00 a.m. in New York, and 7:00 p.m. in Dubai time; I was sleeping when the telephone bell rang; when I got up and picked up the telephone, my daughter Zelgay Ahmed was on the phone from Dubai.

She just said Daddy-Daddy get up and watch CNN when I ran down to the living room and turned on the TV, I saw an unbelievable tragedy and watched the WTC in New York burning down; the ashes covered the whole city, the fire workers and the people in the area covered with dust and ashes of the buildings, screaming, crying, running.

The people of the United States and the world were wondering what happened. And why did it happen? Why did the planes hit the buildings? And who is or who is behind all this inhuman act?

When I heard that was a terrorist act, it was unacceptable to me because, after the tragedy of crashing ill-fated Pan Am Flight 073 on September 5, 1986, in Karachi, in my letter dated September 8th, 1986, addressed to H.E. Mr. Javier Perez de Cuellar, United Nations Secretary-General, and copies were sent to the International Air Transportation Association (IATA). World leaders, I had to warn them that the emergence of terrorism on the surface and air is a hazardous phenomenon and someday would be out of control if the world, especially the world body 'U.N.' and the 'IATA' as well the members of the United Nations don't take strong and decisive action regarding the eradication of terrorism on the surface and in the air. But unfortunately, the U.N. and the world leaders didn't give any attention to my letter.

The IATA assured me in a letter dated October 1ˢᵗ, 1986, saying that "Terrorism is indeed a scourge that we must all combat, and you may be assured the airlines, governments, and airports are cooperating as never before to that end"(See Cry of Afghan page).

Therefore because the assurance was given to me from 'IATA,' I did not believe that would be the act of a person; there must be a group or an organization behind this massive inhuman act for a particular purpose or reason; I was kept asking myself the same question over and over,

Who did it? Why would he do that? Why did it happen right after Ahmed Shah Massud's assassination on the 9ᵗʰ of September, 2001? Is there any connection between September 11 and September 9ᵗʰ happening? And many other questions.

Yet my questions were not answered; a few days after the September 11 tragedy President Bush and the key members of his administration forgot the 3000 innocent people buried under the rubbles of (WTC) the cry of their bereaved ones, the sorrow of Americans and the people of the world, above all his promises to American Nation and the people of the world during the first two, three days of the sad event happened.

They, as a bunch of experienced hunters, like before the tragedy of 9/11, sat in the White House and Pentagon to plan a hunting program for the weekend or later and decide where to go for hunting. And what to hunt?

This time was not the hunting of animals, birds or fishing. It was hunting the human to get the Oil of Iraq or going to Afghanistan to get the gas of Turkmenistan, as well as the opening of a new chapter for the globalization of war against self-created so-called "International terrorism" for implementing his and his predecessors forward policy in the world, predominantly Muslim countries after the defeat of Communism. In the end, once again.

I pray to our God almighty to have the place of all they have lost their precious life in that sad event in Heaven and their soul be in peace. – I express my most profound Sorrow and Condolence to all the bereaved families.

From:- Conspiracies and Atrocities in Afghanistan, 1700-2014(pages 521-522) conclude my cries with the following words, I would like to express with my most profound sorrow that my cries have not been virtual cries such as in my childhood to cry for as changing my wet diaper, feeding me, being too hot, or too cold, had a fever, pain or slapped or pinched by someone on my face or on my body, or not reaching my toys seeking help and etc., or in my adult life I have cried because the loss of my beloved ones in the family, instead all my letters and proposals were my silent cries means my deep internal cries by using pen and paper to express my appeals reflecting mine and my all Afghan, citizens desire to draw the attention of the world leaders including the United Nations, None Aligned movement, Islamic Conference and other world organizations to the crimes, crises, atrocities, destructions, replacing millions of my country men and women out of their beloved motherland such as me and my immediate and extended families members scattered in different parts of the world or displaced inside the country from one province to other and the injustices happening in my beloved motherland in last 44 years since the bloody coup of Hafizullah Amin on April 27, 1987, and murdering the first president of Republic of Afghanistan late Sardar Mohammad Daud Khan, and all his family including his brother Sardar Mohamad Naim Khan, on early morning of April 28,and later in Dec 1979, the open military invasion of the then Soviet Union and installing Babrak Karmal As their Puppet and lost our freedom, independence and National sovereignty. Indeed that was an unbelievable, unfortunate tragedy in the history of Afghanistan; I believed that only the then Soviet Union and Communists were the cruellest atrocities in the world, though, from the pages of the past, history I knew that the non-Communist world was beating up the drum of Communism-O-Phobia since the October Revolution in 1917 in Russia.

However, still, I was very naïve. I wasn't thinking that the Americans and their western allies were beating up the drum of freedom, justice, human rights, and democracy.

They would be worse than the Soviet Union; actually, I admit that I was wrong. It was different. They were too bloodsuckers of the poor but rich under the ground. They were working together to defeat Russia and Communism in the blood of my Afghan citizens, to reach their aims no matter how much it cost them and Afghans, not letting Russia go of the Indian Ocean; after that USA and British invaded Afghanistan on October 7, 2001, on the pretext of freedom and democracy and brought their puppets Hamed Karzai and Dr. Ashraf Ghani one after the other the irony was that both adversaries used my egoistic ignorance of the enemies' conspiracies.

They became the hired servants of the enemies and destroyed their beloved motherland, and lost the independence, national integrity and territorial integrity of the strongest country in the region. Since the defeat of the Soviet Union and Communist the western world using Islamic extremism to reach out to Russia, China, Central Asia and Iran, and in the meantime beating up the Islamophobia Phenomena by their servants, especially Pakistan, so-called Mujahideen, Taliban, Al Qaida and ISIS to destroy Islam on the surface of the earth under the leadership of ISI of Pakistan and bringing the Taliban into power in Afghanistan again. Therefore, the task of my cries in the last 44 years is not over yet; as long as I am alive, my heart will be beating harder and harder for the well-being of my all Afghan brothers and sisters. (Afghan Nation) Though my half heart is not functioning correctly, and I am 84, I will never stop my cries for the cause of my motherland, and I will continue my cries for freedom, independence and national unity. Social justice democracy, to get back the national sovereignty and territorial sovereignty of my beloved motherland Afghanistan in non-violent ways, is my promise; I am sure my heroic Afghan Nation would do the same. God help us.

CONCLUSION

I conclude my cries with an important message. I would like to emphasize and express with my most profound sorrow that my cries have not been empty, such as the cries of a baby with a wet diaper, an empty stomach, or a fever. Similarly, only I have cried or shed tears in my adult life for the loss of my beloved ones in the family. Instead, all my letters and proposals were my silent cries, my deep internal cries using pen and paper to express my appeals and plead with the world leaders to bring an end to the massacre in my motherland to have peaceful, free, independent and democratic Afghanistan.

My cries reflect the desire of all Afghan citizens to draw the attention of the world leaders, including the United Nations, Nonaligned Movement, Islamic Conference and other world organizations, to the crimes, crises, atrocities, and destruction in Afghanistan.

They are the cries of millions of my countrymen and women now living away from their beloved motherland, which includes me and my immediate and extended family members scattered in different parts of the world. Some were even displaced inside the country from one province to another.

They are the cries against the injustices happening in my beloved motherland in the last 44 years since the bloody coup of Hafizullah Amin on April 27, 1987, and the murder of the first president of the Republic of Afghanistan, Sardar Mohammad Daud Khan, and all his family. It included his brother Sardar Mohamad Naim Khan, on the early morning of April 28, followed later in Dec 1979 by the open military invasion of the Soviet Union, who eventually installed Babrak Karmal as their puppet leader. It resulted in the loss of our freedom, independence and national sovereignty.

Indeed that was an unbelievable, unfortunate tragedy in the history of Afghanistan. I believed that only the Soviet Union and Communists were capable of the cruellest atrocities in the world, though, from the pages of history, I know that the non-communist world has been beating the drum of Communism-O-Phobia since the October Revolution in 1917 in Russia.

However, I was still very naïve. I thought that the Americans and their western allies were beating the drum of freedom, justice, human rights, and democracy. They ended up being worse than the Soviet Union. So, I admit that I was wrong.

They, too, were the bloodsuckers of developing countries that are rich in underground resources. They were working together to defeat Russia and communism in the blood of my Afghan citizens to reach their aims no matter how much it cost them and Afghans. They would not let Russia go off the Indian Ocean.

They also with the collaboration of Pakistan and Arab countries brought the so-called Mujaheddin into power in 1992, destroyed Kabul City, Killed more than 75000 innocent Kabul residents and give away most of the arms and ammunition including Tanks and aeroplanes to Pakistan free or destroyed them in the civil war.

Still, they were not satisfied they brought the Taliban in 1996 under the leadership of Bin Laden to destroy the civilization and move Afghanistan, back to the Stone Age.

After the sad incident of September 11, the USA and Britain invaded Afghanistan on October 7, 2001, on the pretext of freedom and democracy throwing out the Taliban and bringing their puppets, such as Hamed Karzai and Dr. Ashraf Ghani, one after the other. The irony was that both of them didn't learn from previous puppets who were also used as their hired servants to destroy their motherland as a result they lost the independence, national integrity and territorial integrity of the strongest country in the region.

Since the defeat of the Soviet Union and Communists, the western world has been using Islamic extremism to reach out to Russia, China, Central Asia and Iran.

In the meantime, they have been heating the Islam-o-phobia phenomena by encouraging their servants, especially Pakistan, the so-called Mujahideen, the Taliban, Al Qaida and ISIS, to try to destroy true and moderate Islam on the surface of the earth under the leadership of ISI of Pakistan to bring the Taliban into power in Afghanistan once again.

Therefore, the task of my cries in the last 44 years is not over yet. As long as I am alive, my heart will be beating harder and harder for the well-being of all my Afghan brothers and sisters and the Afghan Nation. Though my half heart is not functioning correctly, and I am 85, I will never stop my cries and appeals for the cause of my beloved motherland. I will continue my cries and appeals for freedom, independence, national unity, social justice, democracy, and national and territorial sovereignty in nonviolent ways. That is my promise. I am sure my heroic Afghan Nation would do the same. God help us.

THE END BUT NOT ENDED
(back cover continuation)

Afghanistan is one of the Islamic countries in the south Asian region with lots of underground wealth and a strategic position. Therefore, for all Afghans and Muslim nations, in particular, the Islamic scholars, is necessary to wake up and redefine Islam with a new vision of the social, economic, and political structure of the world as well as the development of new technology and the making of sophisticated arms in the world which were not available 1400 years ago. I understand, and by heart, I believe that the Holy Quran is the last Holly book, adaptable and flexible in all situations up to the end of the world. Therefore, it is the job of all Muslim scholars to wake up and think scholarly with open eyes to define Islam according to the true definition of Sharia, especially respecting other religions and the equal rights between men and women in all aspects of life, given the situation in the 21st century and after. Therefore, the Islamic Conference needs to give a universal adaptable definition and guideline of Islam in vital issues to the United Nations that all Muslim countries should act the same. Furthermore, the Muslim scholars, along with the other non-Muslim scholars, should establish a definition for terrorism, terrorist and the act of terrorism on the surface of the earth and the air. That also should be submitted to the United Nations and be adopted universally. If these two things are adopted, Islam-o-Phobia globally will be stopped. Then, hopefully, peace will prevail globally, especially in Afghanistan and all Muslim countries. Therefore, I seek God's help to achieve our sacred goals to see peace in the world and an independent, peaceful and prosperous Afghanistan in my life.

CPSIA information can be obtained
at www.ICGtesting.com
Printed in the USA
BVHW022304091122
651633BV00002B/11